NATURE'S GREAT MIGRATIONS

NATURE'S GREAT MIGRATIONS

AMAZING ANIMAL JOURNEYS FROM AROUND THE WORLD

Marianne Taylor

Contents

Introduction

Some of us love to travel, while others would rather stay at home. Nearly all of us would agree, though, that the actual process of travelling is a bit of a bore. The packing, the waiting, the unpacking. Depending how you choose to travel, you might have to worry about sea-sickness, a restrictive baggage allowance, missing your connection because of the wrong kind of leaves on the line, or running out of petrol. Depending where you go, you may have to fill in a mountain of forms, or learn a new language, or invest in a whole new wardrobe. As you wait to board your plane or train or boat or hovercraft, you might glance up at swallows flying overhead, free of every one of these concerns as they embark on their own long-haul journey, and think, 'alright for you'. You might think again if you knew how many of those swallows would never actually make it to their intended destination.

For an animal, the ability to move is a double-edged sword. You have freedom, but you also have dilemmas. At any given moment, for all kinds of reasons, you might be better off in place B than place A. However, getting from A to B might carry risks, sometimes very considerable ones. Should you stay or should you go?

Glance across the animal kingdom and you'll find plenty that opt to stay. Sea animals like barnacles, some molluscs and sea anemones start out life as free-swimming larvae, but once they settle on the sea bed they are literally rooted to the spot until they die (and some of these organisms live for many years). We often envy birds their ability to take to the skies and go wherever they please – but some birds, such as the Tawny Owl, aren't remotely interested in exploring the world, and never roam more than a couple of kilometres from their birthplace. If your immediate environment meets all your needs then why move? You do have to cross your fingers (or claws, or tentacles…), though, that your immediate environment doesn't suddenly change for the worse.

Why migrate?

We live in a world of contrasts. Those of us who live at particularly northerly or southerly latitudes are acutely aware of the contrast between winter and summer. As I write, it is February and Britain is enduring a particularly cold snap. Small birds like Eurasian Wrens and Goldcrests are struggling – they have to eat almost constantly to keep the fierce little fires of their metabolism burning hotly enough to stave off the cold, and the insects they need are hard to find when everything is veiled in frost. Most of the other British insect-eating birds, though, are doing fine because they're not here – they left for southern Europe or Africa last autumn and won't be back for a couple more months.

But did the ancestors of these migratory birds live here year-round somehow, or did they originally live

Opposite: We tend to think of sea anemones as the ultimate sedentary creature, but in the early stages of life they can travel long distances as larvae.

Page 2: Christmas Island Red Crab.

Pages 4–5: Arctic Tern.

year-round much further south? The latter scenario is most likely. Africa is home to dozens of species of swallows and martins, more than anywhere in the world, strongly suggesting that swallows first evolved in Africa. Most of the African species are sedentary. Only three members of this group come to Britain and breed, and they spend their winters in Africa. Over many millennia, their ancestors moved further and further north to breed, taking advantage of longer daylight hours and much less competition from other birds. But they couldn't stay all year, because the flipside of those long warm summer days is very short, very cold winter days and a dearth of insects to eat.

For other animals, the motivation to move is the same – at some times of the year it's better to be at A than B, and at other times B is better than A. Usually this is down to changes in food availability, but may also be driven by a limited number of places to breed. Seals and seabirds usually need safe offshore islands to have their young. Many butterflies and moths can only lay their eggs on one particular kind of plant, and where and when they travel is controlled by when and where that plant can be found in its most optimal condition. The alternative to migration is inactivity during the lean times – hibernation or aestivation. This suits animals that are not very mobile, but it carries its own risks and challenges, and for many, migration is a better option.

Nevertheless, the dangers of migration may be considerable. Often the route means crossing hostile terrain, where food is scarce and dangers are plentiful. However, in a world that is transforming at an extraordinary rate, the travellers may well have the upper hand over the stay-at-homers. We are already seeing changes in migratory routes and behaviour, which seem to be in response to human activities. 'Adapt or die' is a motto that applies as much to animal life as to our own.

Defining migration

Migration in its strictest form is a regular, predictable seasonal movement. In the tropics, this may mean moving in rhythm with the rainy and dry seasons, and may be driven as much by the need to find water as food. For very mobile sea animals, moving around may be guided by prevailing ocean currents, and for sea animals that produce lots of young and also have cannibalistic tendencies, travelling a lot is a good way to help ensure you don't accidentally eat too many of your own offspring. For animals that live in the mountains, migration may be a short but vital trip a few hundred metres downslope when winter bites – this is altitudinal migration.

When animals move unpredictably and en masse, this is known as irruption. It is usually driven by food, or rather a lack of food. Animals that rely on a fluctuating food source can cope in lean years by moving away

Many species of swallows migrate relatively short distances compared to the Barn Swallow. For example, the White-throated Swallow (pictured) breeds in South Africa and migrates to Zambia and Angola outside the breeding season.

from home, but in good years they can stay put. Sometimes when a population reaches a certain 'critical mass', this triggers a mass movement away to new areas, before competition for resources becomes too severe.

Finding the way

Perhaps the most intriguing aspect of animal migration concerns how they know where to go – and when. While some may learn the way from their parents, many animals migrate alone rather than in family groups, and youngsters have to navigate unaided when they make their first journey. Migratory animals tend to have a genetic predisposition to move in a particular direction when certain environmental conditions occur, such as changing day length and air temperature, or a change in the weather. These same cues can tell it when the destination has been reached and it's time to stop. Migrating animals may navigate by sensing the Earth's magnetic field and determining their changing position relative to it, or by noting changes in the positions of the Sun or stars as they move – or they may simply be carried along by prevailing winds or currents. Real-life experience does play an important role in long-lived migrators, though. Older animals that have migrated many times make increasing use of landmarks to refine their route, and learn how to use the vagaries of the weather to their advantage, while first-time migrators are far more likely to go off-course and get themselves hopelessly lost.

The adventurers

This book takes a close look at a selection of the world's most notable migratory animals – the ones undertaking the longest, most challenging or most bizarre journeys of all. They range from whales to wildebeest, terns to turtles, and bats to butterflies. Some fly, some swim, others run, walk or scuttle, but all have earned their right to be known as the greatest travellers on earth. We examine the animal itself – its biology and ecology, how it leads its life and why it migrates. Then we journey with it on its migration, exploring what we've learned of how, where and when it travels, and what mysteries remain to be uncovered.

Opposite: Painted Lady butterflies are
famed for their long-distance migrations.

Grey Whale

Eschrichtius robustus

IUCN Least Concern

In our watery world, big sea animals have tremendous freedom of movement. The biggest of all sea animals – indeed of all animals, ever – are the great whales, and nearly all of them are great travellers. Wherever they go they are a vital part of marine ecology – by feeding in deep water and defecating at the surface they move nutrients up through the water column, benefiting many species of fish and seabirds, and when they die and their vast corpses sink to the sea-bed, they feed so many species for such a long time that entire miniature ecosystems form around their bodies. Baleen whales lack teeth, instead having sieve-like plates in their mouths that filter out the planktonic sea animals – the array of tiny amphipods, isopods, copepods, fish fry and much more – on which they feed.

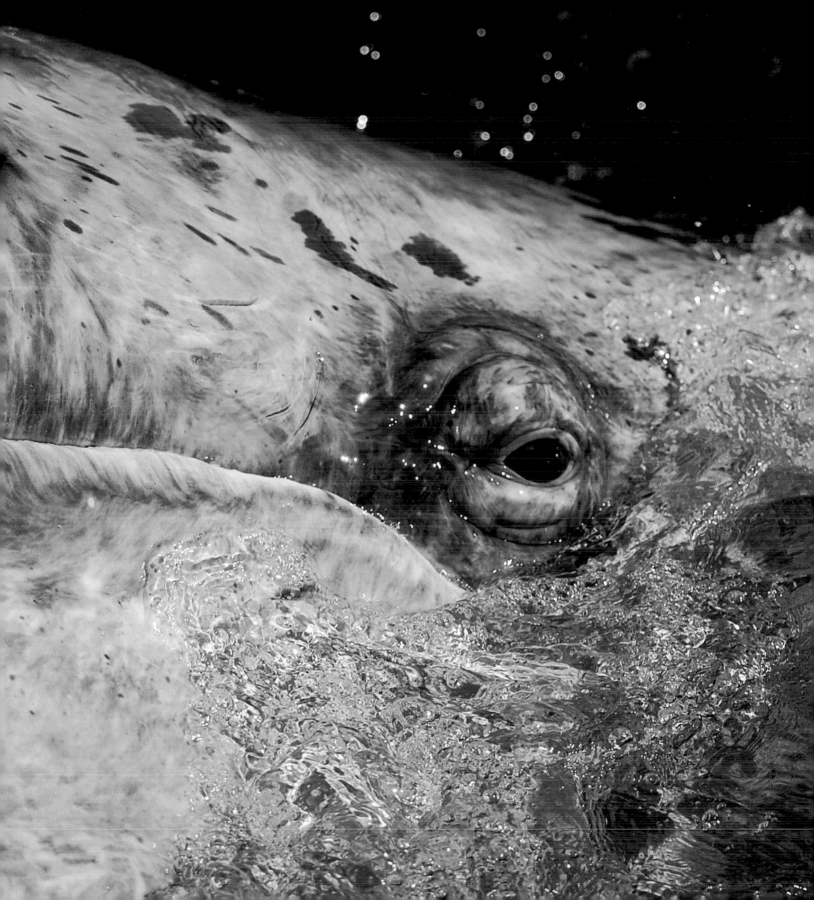

The traveller

The Grey Whale is a largish, rather blunt-headed and stocky-bodied baleen whale, the biggest individuals (which are females) growing to nearly 15m (50ft) long and weighing more than 30 tons. Grey Whales can live into their 60s or 70s. This species has no dorsal fin, but a 'dorsal hump' close to its tail; it has a double blow-hole and proportionately rather small fins and flukes. The grey skin is crusted here and there with barnacles, patched white in places where whale lice set up home, and often marked with scrapes and scars from near-misses with Killer Whales (its only natural predator) – these distinguishing marks make it relatively easy for biologists to identify different individuals. It is the only species in its genus, and feeds on the sea-bed rather than in deeper and more open water, tilting itself onto one side to scoop up mouthfuls of sediment, from which it sifts tiny crustaceans. Its preference for feeding inshore led to its' being nicknamed 'the friendly whale'. Because its feeding method means it often bumps its head on the sea-bed, it becomes more scarred on one side of the head than the other (usually the right side) and older individuals may suffer loss of sight in the eye on that side.

Like other great whales, Grey Whales suffered tremendously at the hands of whalers, despite being considered a rather sub-standard whale, its baleen and oil of poor quality compared to other species like the Bowhead and Northern Right Whales. Much of the hunting took place in Magdalena Bay and Scammon's Lagoon in Baja California, Mexico. It came close to extinction and was completely eradicated from large parts of its range before it gained legal protection in the USA in 1936, and commercial whaling as a whole was drastically scaled back in the mid-20th century. The whalers gave it a new nickname – 'devil fish' – because it was such a fierce fighter when harpooned. This behaviour had a lot to do with the fact that whalers preferred to target females that had recently calved. The calves were not desirable to the whalers but those that survived the hunt soon starved without their mothers.

Prior to commercial whaling, the world population was probably more than 100,000 individuals (this is an estimate based on the genetic diversity of the species today). Today, there are thought to be about 20,000–25,000 Grey Whales, representing a significant recovery from late 19th-century population levels, and the species is no longer considered endangered. Most of these are in the eastern Pacific, but there is also a tiny subpopulation of some 100–120 animals in the western Pacific. These differ anatomically from the eastern animals in various ways, and could be a distinct subspecies. The Atlantic population was completely wiped out by commercial whaling but recently a handful of individuals have been seen outside the Pacific.

Opposite: A Grey Whale shows its baleen plates, the structures that allow it to filter huge volumes of tiny prey from seawater.

Overleaf: A whale-watcher's dream – a Grey Whale breaches almost fully clear of the water.

The journey

Grey Whales in the north Pacific begin their migration in mid-autumn, as Arctic ice spreads southwards. Their route hugs the Pacific coastline of North America, all the way down to their calving grounds close to the coast of Baja California. The whales travel in particular age and sex classes, with pregnant mature females leading the way. Not far behind are males, along with females in oestrus and in search of a mate, while the youngsters (seven years old and under) follow along behind. The journey of some 8,000km (5,000 miles) takes about three months, and there are ample opportunities for whale-watchers on land to enjoy the spectacle of these great animals on the move through the winter months. During migration, Grey Whales can cover 120km (75 miles) a day and when in travel mode they move at an average of 8km/h (5mph). They feed if they can but are mainly sustained by fat stores laid down in the summer.

The whales assemble in shallow bays and lagoons, and here calves are born and romances are pursued. Males and newly mated females don't stay very long, heading back on the long northward swim towards the Bering Sea and nearby as early as February. Females with calves linger for longer in the safe, sheltered lagoons, and may not depart until May. Calves feed from their mothers for about seven months, but the lengthy pregnancy of 13.5 months means that females produce young only every two years.

The tiny western Pacific population spends the summer in the Sea of Okhotsk, off Sakhalin island in the far north-east of Russia, but little is known of where they go in winter. There is historical evidence that they moved down the coast of eastern Asia to winter off China, thanks to infrequent observations and discoveries of dead whales caught in fishing nets, but no definite gathering place for mating and calving had ever been discovered.

Because these whales are so few in number and may constitute a distinct subspecies, scientists have been keen to learn more about their migratory routes, and several animals have been fitted with satellite tags to

track their journeys. The results of these studies are quite startling – the western whales no longer seem to stick to 'their' side of the Pacific, but are moving over to the American coastline, where they probably come into direct contact with the eastern Pacific population. One particular whale, a female named 'Varvara', covered an epic 22,000km (13,700 miles) in 2011–12 in a migratory round-trip between Sakhalin and Baja California. This is the longest mammal migration ever recorded, by a substantial margin, and to achieve it Varvara navigated her way across open sea for considerable parts of the journey, rather than sticking to the coastline all the way as the eastern Pacific whales do.

What does this mean for Grey Whales? At the moment, there are rather more questions than answers. Varvara is a young whale and the duration of her stays in Baja California indicate that she has not yet calved. But if she does seek a mate there in due course, she will encounter far more eastern than western Pacific Grey Whales. Do the two forms interbreed freely? Have they always done so, or is this new behaviour? Do some western Pacific whales still spend the winter in Asia? Or could it be the other way round, and Varvara and her friends are actually eastern Pacific whales that have switched their behaviour to spend summer in Asia? It is the usual mantra – more study needed. But there can be no doubt that Varvara's great journey, its details confirmed beyond all doubt by cutting-edge science, is the stuff of legend.

Map: Grey Whales in the eastern Pacific migrate along the coastline from Alaska down to Mexico and back.

Above: Tourists enjoy a very close encounter with 'the friendly whale'.

Harp Seal

Pagophilus groenlandicus

IUCN Least Concern

In Scotland, Ireland and the Faroe Islands, there are folk tales of 'selkies' – seals who shed their skins to reveal a human form, and come onto land, marrying people and having children with them. But the seals invariably regain their seal-skins and return to the sea in the end, however much they love their human families. Though not as fully aquatic as the whales, seals have little need of land – except to bear their young. When not breeding, many species travel substantial distances to reach the best fishing grounds.

Harp Seal milk is extraordinarily calorific, allowing
the pup to grow rapidly to its 'safe swimmable size'.

The traveller

The Harp Seal's genus name, *Pagophilus*, means 'ice-lover', and aptly sums up the habitat preferences of this beautifully marked animal. It breeds in the High Arctic on the edge of the pack-ice, from east Canada across Greenland to Russia, in three well-separated populations that total about 9 million animals, making this the most abundant seal species in the Northern Hemisphere. There are three key 'herds' or breeding groups – one in the western North Atlantic off North America (the largest by far, holding more than two-thirds of the total population), one around Jan Mayen island east of Greenland, and a third in the White Sea and Barents Sea, Russia.

Harp Seals grow to close to 2m (6.5ft) in length and usually weigh in the region of 130kg (290lb). Mature adults have silvery skin, with darker faces and a dark but pale-centred 'saddle' on their backs, which is shaped a bit like a harp (if you use your imagination). Younger animals are mostly silver with some dark spotting. The newborn pups have a coat of creamy-white fluff, against which their large dark eyes and black noses and muzzles stand out. They are exceptionally endearing – a fact which gave considerable leverage to an ultimately successful 1980s campaign to outlaw 'whitecoat' hunting in Canada, with Russia following suit in 2009. However, older Harp Seals may still be hunted legally.

Harp Seals are adapted to deal with extreme cold right from the start of their lives. The pups are born in late winter, straight onto the pack-ice, but the white infant coat is highly insulating. Pups move very little for the first few weeks of their lives, their body warmth melting a hollow 'ice-cradle' which provides them with some shelter. Though able to swim if necessary from a young age, they mainly avoid the water while they are very small, as they have little or no blubber for warmth and buoyancy. They feed from their mothers for only 12 days, but Harp Seal milk is 60 per cent fat, making this a crash-diet in reverse. Each pup packs on an astounding 2.2kg (4.9lb) every day that it is fed, gaining enough fat to keep it alive through a subsequent six-week fast. The mother, meanwhile, has come into oestrus and leaves her pup behind as she goes off in search of a mate. The pups moult their fluff during their fast, revealing a sleek silver and truly sea-worthy pelage. They become more active as they mature, and play with each other on the ice and in the water. By the time the moult is complete they are spending most of their time in the water and begin to learn how to fish.

These seals are very gregarious and very vocal. They gather in large colonies, several thousand strong, to have their young and then to mate. Hunting is also a social activity, although bigger and older seals make longer and deeper dives. However, the Harp Seal is not a very deep-diving species, rarely going below 100m (330ft) and only occasionally as deep as 300m (990ft), and stays under for about 15 minutes. At the other end of the Earth, the Weddell Seal of the Antarctic can dive to 600m (1,970ft) and stay under for more than an hour, and the elephant seals make even more impressive dives. The Harp Seal is a generalist feeder, known to take 67 different species of fish and 70 species of marine invertebrates. However, it eats a higher proportion of fish in winter, and eats very little through the breeding and moulting period from March to June, consequently losing a great deal of weight.

The journey

Harp Seals' migration is guided by their need to stay close to the Arctic pack-ice where it adjoins open sea. As the ice spreads in winter and retreats in summer, the seals move with it, and individuals may cover distances of 4,000km (2,485 miles) or more. A young Harp Seal that was fitted with a tag as a pup in the Gulf of St Lawrence was recovered some months later off Norway, having travelled 4,640km (2,883 miles). This was prior to the days of satellite-tracking, but uniquely marked tags fitted to a flipper have been used on seals for some decades, in much the same way that birds are marked with unique leg rings.

Because the seals follow the ice, they don't need to modify their behaviour in any particular way as they travel. Their food supply moves with them, and they can haul out and rest on the ice at any time. However, sometimes their migration does go quite dramatically wrong, and there have been a number of incidents in the last few decades when large numbers of Harp Seals have moved far further south than they 'should', and beyond the pack ice. In winter 1987, thousands of Harp Seals from the White Sea area moved well into Norwegian waters, with many travelling inland along fjords, and the following four years also saw unusual numbers off Norway. In the same period, there were records from the Netherlands, Germany and Denmark and northern France. Most of these animals were adult males.

This 'irruption' is thought to have been triggered by food shortages. It coincided with a crash in the population of Capelin, a normally abundant small, oily fish that is an important part of the Harp Seal diet in winter. The seals were emaciated and in generally very poor condition – many were found dead – so a desperate search for food seems to explain all. Capelin numbers recovered in the early 1990s but fell again in the mid-1990s. However, this second crash didn't trigger a significant rush of Harp Seals into more southerly waters – perhaps because their own population was still recovering from the previous disaster, or perhaps they made use of another food source.

Harp Seals are hugely abundant and overall their population is increasing at the moment. In recent years the number taken by hunters has fallen well short of the legal quota (which is several hundred thousand per year). The most serious threat they face, in common with other animals of polar regions, is climate change, which is likely to shrink and fragment their pack-ice habitat in years to come. For animals that are already living at Earth's extremes, there is literally nowhere else to go. In the winter of 2007, the Canadian press reported that both ice and seals were hard to find in the Gulf of St Lawrence, and pup mortality was extremely high. The Harp Seal's willingness to travel thousands of kilometres from its home turf when food is hard to find may make the difference between life and death for individual animals, but without pack-ice on which to bear its young, the species as a whole will be in very serious trouble.

Map: Young Harp Seals are silver with variable black spots. The harp pattern does not appear until the seals reach sexual maturity.

Caribou or Reindeer

Rangifer tarandus

IUCN Least Concern

If what our parents told us on Christmas Eve was true, then this animal would easily win the top spot for furthest *and* fastest migration. Sadly, most of us now know that a team of flying Caribou (or Reindeer, as the species is known in Eurasia) does not stop off at every household on Earth over the course of just one night. Some Caribou *are* great travellers, but they make their way across the inhospitable and sometimes treacherous Arctic tundra and taiga on foot, over many weeks, one steady step at a time.

Caribou migration is guided by the need for
good grazing and browsing at all times of year.

The traveller

Caribou are heavy but relatively short-legged and stocky deer, built to conserve rather than to lose their body heat. Mature animals have complex and multi-spiked antlers – spindly in the most northerly Caribou but extremely big, heavy and almost bushy-looking in others. As with other big deer, the males are often known as 'bulls' and the females as 'cows'. Young Caribou are 'calves'.

Uniquely among deer, antlers are sported by both sexes (although females' are generally smaller and in a few populations females are antler-less). They have thick coats, including a 'ruff' around their necks, and broad 'snow-shoe' feet, and are decked out in a mainly black-and-silver pelage. Many become whiter in the winter months, and have a shorter and darker coat through summer. Their hooves also change through the seasons. The pads on the soles of their 'summer feet' are thick and spongy, providing traction on boggy ground. In winter the pads contract, exposing the sharp edges of the hooves, which are used to dig through snow to reach the lichens they eat. No other mammal habitually eats lichen – Caribou have a specialised gut flora that allows them to extract the nutrients from this challenging foodstuff.

Across the whole of the Arctic, there are many different subspecies of Caribou, and they vary considerably in size, antler size and prevailing colour. Generally more northerly forms, living on tundra rather than in woodland, are bigger and paler, and more extravagantly antlered. They are rather laid-back as deer go, and in much of their range they are semi-domesticated, providing Arctic communities like the Sami in Scandinavia with a source of meat, milk, hide and labour. The communities who 'keep' them do not generally contain them in any way but do herd them, moving the animals between summer and winter camps as required. Some of these journeys even involve short sea crossings to pasture-rich islands – Caribou are strong swimmers, though the herders prefer to travel by canoe.

The journey

Some Caribou are not strictly migratory at all, although they roam nomadically as their need for food dictates. Others do make regular migrations between traditional wintering and summer grounds. One particular subspecies undertakes the longest on-foot migration of any animal on earth. This is the Porcupine Caribou (*Rangifer tarandus granti*), named because it lives in the vicinity of the Porcupine River that runs through Alaska and western Canada. The Porcupine Caribou herd is about 169,000-strong – a number determined through aerial photography. It is one of the large, massive-antlered tundra forms, with males weighing in at up to 300kg (660lb).

These deer travel about 2,400km (1,500 miles) each year, moving between winter feeding areas and the calving grounds. On the way, they cross spongy bog-land, snow-fields and mountainous areas, and they even ford fast-flowing rivers. The winter grounds are in the south of their range, and in summer they move to the northern coastal plain where the females give birth to their calves. The precise route they take, though, varies from year to year and is dictated by conditions on the ground – serious flooding or late heavy snow can render areas impassable even for these strong swimmers and broad-footed walkers. If forced to take a series of 'long-way-round' detours to avoid problem areas, they may walk more than 4,000km (2,485 miles) in a year.

Pregnant females lead the way on the northbound spring migration, setting off in April and arriving at the beginning of June. They move quite briskly, covering some 20km (12 miles) a day. Within a couple of weeks the rest have arrived and the entire herd is spread across the coastal plain, making the most of the short, intense Arctic summer before they begin to disperse, as early as mid-July. They roam about in the north, sometimes covering even more kilometres per day as they look for areas of good forage and low numbers of biting insects, often finding what they need on high ground. They start to head southwards as the weather worsens through early autumn. On the way, the rut takes place, when the biggest of the bulls compete for access to the adult cows in spectacular antler-clashing contests, and mating occurs. After the rut, the deer shed their antlers and begin to grow a new and larger set.

Throughout the winter months the herd tends to keep on the move in the search for food. At this time of year it is not plentiful pasture, but sparse lichens which they get at by scraping away snow with their hooves. However, with the rigours of the rut (for males) and feeding calves (for females) now behind them, with a bit of luck the deer can thrive and gain weight through winter. They do have to contend with predators, in particular wolves and to a lesser extent bears, which follow the herds all through autumn, winter and spring.

Weaker deer – particularly the young calves born that summer, but also mature bulls exhausted from the rut, and any animals carrying injury – are targeted by the predators. Bears often assemble at traditional river crossing points, ready to attack any deer that get into difficulties negotiating the crossing. Only on the calving grounds are the deer free of the predators' attention, because the open coastal plains offer no suitable denning areas for wolves and bears to have their own young.

These animals have a long and intimate history with the Gwinch'in, an indigenous people of Alaska and Canada, whose traditional settlements reflect the Porcupine Caribou's preferred migratory routes, although it was always taboo to hunt or even go near the animals on their calving grounds. A number of other indigenous people also hunt the deer, and the herd's numbers are managed for sustainability and to avoid excessive disturbance by the Alaska Department of Fish and Game and Canadian wildlife agencies, as well as the local people who hunt them. Their economic value goes beyond supplying meat and skins – they are also a significant tourist attraction with tour companies offering trips for photographers and wildlife-watchers centred around witnessing the spectacle.

The deer wander over a huge area, which includes some national parks and refuges. Most notably, part of their calving grounds is in the Arctic National Wildlife Refuge in Alaska, which at just over 78,000 sq km (30,100 sq miles) is the largest national wildlife refuge in the USA. Recent proposals to permit drilling for oil on the refuge would be likely to have a serious impact on this remarkable and economically important animal.

Map: The Porcupine herd moves north in summer just before the females calve.

Blue Wildebeest

Connochaetes taurinus

IUCN Least Concern

Thanks to decades of ever more dazzling wildlife documentaries on TV, most of us are very familiar with the great migrations of the African grazing mammals. No animal is more likely to be described as 'sweeping across the plains' than the Blue Wildebeest, aka Brindled Gnu, and the many terrible hazards that it faces as it travels are shown to us in graphic, often gory detail. However, the sheer scale of the moving herds and the many obstacles that they do overcome also brings home the message of migration as an unstoppable force.

Wildebeest herds move like fast-flowing water, and quickly find the most efficient routes across difficult terrain.

The traveller

Although it looks rather like a slightly oddly proportioned cow, this animal is actually an antelope. Like all antelopes it belongs to the cow family (Bovidae) but is a member of the subfamily Alcelaphinae, a grouping of similarly stocky, front-heavy, doleful-looking antelopes with long faces and usually small and back-curved horns. Relatives of the Blue Wildebeest include the hartebeests, the Topi and its closest cousin, the Black or White-tailed Wildebeest, which replaces it in southernmost Africa. The word 'wildebeest' comes from the Afrikaans for 'wild beast', while 'gnu' describes the animal's dour mooing call.

The Blue Wildebeest is a silver-blue animal with obscure pale stripes on its body, and a darker face and legs. Its front-heavy look is exaggerated by its mane, running down between its shoulders to the middle of its back, and beard. It has a thick neck and heavy shoulders but rather slight hindquarters and spindly-looking legs, and a long tasselled tail that swishes about wildly when the animal is running. Its peculiar appearance has led to the unflattering suggestion that it was built from bits of other local animals – the sloping-backed body of a hyena balanced on spindly antelope legs, with a Giraffe's tail at one end and a baboon's long face, surmounted by Cape Buffalo horns, at the other.

It looks ungainly whether walking or going at full tilt, with a strange rocking motion, but it has good endurance and can reach close to 70km/h (43mph) in full flight. A healthy adult wildebeest can run fast enough and for long enough to escape most potential predators, as long as it sees them in time to accelerate to its top speed. It lives in sub-Saharan Africa and is highly gregarious, living and travelling in herds thousands or tens of thousands strong. Members of the herd are quite vocal, staying in touch with frequent low-pitched moos, while territorial males are even noisier.

Life in a huge and endlessly travelling herd is marked by such phenomena as the highly synchronised birth of calves – 80–90 per cent are born within the same three-week window. Many calves are lost to predators when still very small and vulnerable, despite the best efforts of their mothers to keep them protected in the middle of the herd. However, there is such a glut of calves that the predators can only make a small dent in the total numbers before the babies reach an age and size where they are no longer such easy prey. Coping with predators – from Lions to Nile Crocodiles and Wild Dogs to Leopards, is a fact of life for wildebeests, but living in a big herd makes the task difficult for the hunters, as they try to isolate one animal from a great rushing mass. Weaker and slower animals are more likely to be targeted, with the fast and strong surviving attack after attack, week in week out, and becoming a little wilier and harder to catch with every escape. If a wildebeest gets through its early months and is lucky enough to stay fit and healthy, it can live to be 15 or 20 years old.

Like most big, social grazing mammals, the males hold territory and compete for the right to mate, and females only choose to mate with the 'best' combatants. Males' territories have to be redefined as the herd moves around. For social reasons like this, the herds are not of uniform composition – pregnant and nursing

Above: With danger lurking in the river, the wildebeests make the crossing at full speed.

Opposite: Space and good grazing – the reward for the struggle of migration.

females stick together, and so do juveniles that are independent of their mothers but too young to breed. Males also gather in herds until they are seeking to mate, and then become territorial.

The journey

The range of the Blue Wildebeest is extensive, covering a large swathe of sub-Saharan Africa. Some populations are sedentary, but wildebeests in the Serengeti area of east Africa are serious long-distance migrants, covering hundreds of kilometres as they move around to find water sources and the best grazing. They are accompanied by smaller (but still impressive) numbers of other grazers, including Burchell's Zebra, a valuable ally to the wildebeests as it eats taller, tougher grass, making the wildebeests' preferred grass layer more accessible to them. Thomson's and Grant's Gazelles, Impala and Eland also associate with the herds. In all, somewhere around 2 million animals are on the move, more than a million of them Blue Wildebeests. The journey is a long loop that can cover more than 2,000km (1,240 miles) in a year, and it goes on through the year with pauses of from one to three months before it's time to move on again.

Female wildebeests have their calves in late January and February, while in the southern Serengeti. The youngsters can keep up with their seniors within days, which is just as well as the rainy season comes to an end and the herds begin to spread out. By April they are heading resolutely north and westwards. By late

The looping migration of the Serengeti wildebeests is guided by the availability of grazing grounds and waterholes.

summer they are well north, moving towards the Maasai Mara, and this is the time that the dangerous river crossings take place. In late autumn the rainy season begins again and the animals head back south. Their route varies according to local conditions, and migration may stop and start unpredictably, with the herds turning back on themselves at times. In one year they may take one month to cross a particular area, and three months the following year.

Getting across the rivers is a major challenge, yielding much dramatic television footage of deadly Nile Crocodile attacks on the hapless-looking wildebeests as they struggle through the rushing water, and skid and scramble their way up the steep and slippery mudbanks on the other side. Nearly all the wildebeests will survive crossing after crossing though – their numbers overwhelm the predators, and they also employ what's known as 'swarm intelligence' to quickly find the fastest and safest crossing point, and to switch to a new point if the first becomes unsafe.

Predators have been a fact of wildebeest life for countless millennia, and over this time hunters and hunted have evolved – and continue to evolve – in concert. Natural selection ensures that as predators get better at catching prey, so prey gets better at evading predators, increment by tiny increment. However, when change comes too quickly and too extensively, this evolutionary mechanism can't keep up, and disaster may ensue. Spread of human populations took away wildebeest grazing areas, and the livestock that replaced them also spread disease to the wild animals. Hunting on a large scale is another factor, and fencing to contain livestock has caused serious harm to migratory wildebeests, blocking their route and causing mass die-offs in drought years, as the animals couldn't reach water or good grazing. The Maasai Mara area lost about 80 per cent of its Blue Wildebeests between 1977 and 1997.

Today, wildebeest numbers have bounced back somewhat, and the population is stable and not considered to be of immediate conservation concern. The general trend, though, is that the sedentary populations are doing better than the migrants, particularly in protected areas in southern Africa where the animals can meet their needs all year round without having to leave the game reserves. The great wildebeest migrations of east Africa are a tremendous tourist draw, but effectively protecting the entire area used by the animals through the year is almost impossible, so they may always be more vulnerable.

Mexican Free-tailed Bat

Tadarida brasiliensis

IUCN Least Concern

Around the Northern Hemisphere, small songbirds spend their summer daytimes eating insects, and when night falls, the bats take over. And when summer ends and insects become hard to find, most of those small songbirds migrate thousands of kilometres south and spend winter in other lands, eating other insects. Those that don't migrate either switch to a vegetarian diet, or they become ultra-specialists, finding ways to access the few kinds of invertebrate prey that aren't completely out of their reach. The bats, though, have a different tactic – they go to sleep, whiling away the cold months in a state of vastly slowed-down metabolism, and emerge from hibernation in spring when prey is back in abundance. True migration is rare among bats, but in one species it provides one of the greatest spectacles in the natural world.

The traveller

Bats can be divided into two distinct groups – the generally smaller insectivores or Microchiroptera, which occur almost worldwide and find their insect prey through echolocation, and the usually larger 'fruit bats' or Megachiroptera, which are vegetarian, restricted to the tropics, and have no echolocation. The Mexican or Brazilian Free-tailed Bat is an example of the former. It is medium-sized with large broad ears and small eyes, the complex facial anatomy typical of an echolocating bat, and a short, wrinkly-lipped snout concealing a mouthful of tiny sharp teeth. It has relatively long and narrow wings, making it capable of powerful, fast flight,

and as the name suggests its thin tail is long and partly free of the flight membranes that span from wing-tip to toe-tip, and toe-tip to wing-tip.

This animal is a typical insectivorous nocturnal bat, finding its way and its dinner by sound rather than sight. It hunts high in the sky, higher than most other bats, and preys mainly on moths but also other night-flying insects such as beetles. When hunting, it emits a constant stream of calls at a steady frequency, listening for echoes which flag up both obstacles in its path and potential prey. When it is homing in on prey its calls

take on a modulated frequency of between 25–75 kHz. The complexity of its calls is quite mind-boggling. Researchers have identified 14 different calls with a social function, and it is also capable of 'anti-social' calls – it can 'jam' the echolocation calls of other bat species, reducing their hunting success and encouraging them to go elsewhere. All of the frequencies it uses are outside normal human hearing range, but the advent of bat dectector devices has opened up the astonishing sound-world in which this and other bats live, and revealed the complexity of their language.

Mexican Free-tailed Bats are very widespread, their range reaching halfway up the USA, and down through Central America to well into Chile and Argentina, although they are absent from the most heavily

forested parts of South America. They also occur widely in the Caribbean. About nine subspecies are recognised across the species' entire range. Working out the total population of such a widely distributed species is difficult, but the current estimate is that there are in the region of 100 million individuals. Individual roosts can hold more than a million bats – this is a highly social species. With such overwhelming numbers, the bats have economic importance – they consume vast quantities of insects, including many crop pests, and produce vast amounts of guano which is harvested for use as a fertiliser.

The bats' summer breeding colonies are much larger than most winter gatherings. The same sites are used year after year, and some attract hundreds of human visitors to enjoy the spectacle of vast numbers of bats streaming out of the roost at dusk – most famously at Congress Avenue Bridge in Austin, Texas, where 1.5 million bats draw in 100,000 tourists each year. Males and females meet at the summer sites to mate, and then the males leave for smaller 'bachelor' roosts. A female's pregnancy lasts about 12 weeks, and the single infant remains in the roost, in a creche with countless other babies, while its mother is out foraging. She finds her own baby in the crowd on her return by picking up its unique scent and vocalisations – although others that are not her own will try to latch onto her as she clambers among them, making her way towards her own offspring. In the case of the famous Bracken Cave roost in central Texas, a mind-boggling 20 million mother bats have to find their own baby among 19,999,999 others, each night through each summer, every year. The young bats grow very quickly, thanks to consuming a quarter of their bodyweight in high-fat milk every 24 hours, and are independent at between four and seven weeks old – ready to begin their first migration in late summer or early autumn.

Map: The most northerly-breeding Mexican Free-tailed Bats are long-distance migrants.

The journey

While some Mexican Free-tailed Bats do not migrate, and for others seasonal movements are not well-known, those that live in the USA are known to be mostly long-distance migrants, heading south for the winter. Those in central states head for southern Texas and northern Mexico, while many of those in the western USA go to Baja California. The longest documented single journey was 1,777km (1,104 miles) – a bat banded in north-west Oklahoma and recovered in Mexico. Most migrants will cover more than 1,000km (620 miles) on each migration. Those in the far east and far west of the USA make only short-distance movements, while those in at least some parts of the Caribbean are sedentary.

Conditions in the bats' breeding caves become quite unbearable for human visitors, with vast amounts of bacteria and scavenging invertebrates munching their way through the great pungent tonnage of bat guano and occasional dead baby bat. Combined with the stinking air is a stiflingly high temperature, rising to over 35°C (95°F) with the body heat of all those fast-growing bat babies. The adult bats foraging outside, though, could have the opposite problem, as they fly in cool air, hundreds of metres high. Migrants must cope with even colder air as they may travel at as much as 3,000m (9,850ft) above ground level. The ability to contend with a wide range of temperature shifts and remain active is one of the adaptations that allows this bat to make long-distance migrations. Studies have shown that it has much higher thermal efficiency than the non-migratory bats that share its habitat, thanks to the arrangement of blood vessels in the body-sides, adjacent to the wings. These areas of the body can quickly lose heat when necessary but can also hang onto it, by constriction of the blood vessels.

On migration, the bats may make temporary use of less-than-ideal roosting spots. Anywhere sheltered will do – buildings of all kinds, small caves, even hollow trees. They travel in groups and will listen for the calls of other bats to locate roost sites. The full journey, though, can be accomplished very quickly, as on a good night a bat could potentially cover 500km (310 miles) in just a few hours, flying high and fast and perhaps exploiting swarms of moths that are also migrating.

There is much to be discovered about Mexican Free-tailed Bat migration – how they navigate, which routes they take, how flocks are formed and whether associations endure through the winter and summer, why they fly so high, and whether or not those in South America are even greater travellers than their northern counterparts. The most modern satellite trackers are small enough for even these tiny mammals to carry, and we are poised to learn far more about the travels of these and other migratory bats.

Barn Swallow

Hirundo rustica

IUCN Least Concern

The old saying warns us that 'one swallow doesn't make a summer' – acknowledging that the arrival of the Barn Swallow is a sign that spring is here, even if the warmer weather isn't. The quote seems to have come originally from Greek philosopher Aristotle, but is relevant across most of the Northern Hemisphere, because this is a very widely distributed bird. Before anything was known of bird migration, Europeans knew that their swallows and some other birds went missing in winter, but it was believed for many centuries that they hibernated out of sight, perhaps even underwater. The notion of migration was not widely accepted until 1797, when Thomas Bewick mentioned in his *History of British Birds* a report from a sailor who had observed thousands of swallows flying north through the Mediterranean in late winter. Barn Swallow migration to southern Africa was confirmed beyond doubt in December 1912, when a chick ringed in Staffordshire, England, was recovered some months later in Natal, South Africa.

For this highly aerial bird, even delivering
food to its young can be done on the wing.

The traveller

The swallow family contains more than 80 species, of which the Barn Swallow is the m[...]
It breeds in a broad band right across Eurasia and North America, and winters in an equally [...]
the Southern Hemisphere. If we take into account its summer and winter ranges and the area[...] on
migration, there are very few places on Earth away from the poles that are not overflown by Barn Swallows
on a regular basis – the IUCN lists it as 'native' to more than 200 countries.

This is a small and highly aerial bird, with long pointed wings and a long forked tail, and relatively tiny,
puny legs and feet, because it doesn't have very much to do with terra firma. It has a short bill but a wide,
bristle-lined mouth, ideal for hoovering up insects on the wing. A similar body shape can be found in various
unrelated birds such as swifts and nightjars, in a striking example of convergent evolution – their body plan
(particularly in swifts) is quite an extreme departure from the standard small bird 'template' but works so well
that nature invented it anew several times.

Barn Swallows prefer to nest within some kind of sheltering structure – caves and tree hollows would have
been used originally, but buildings that are used infrequently by humans (and that have a swallow-friendly
permanent way in and out) suit their needs perfectly. Thus the Barn Swallow has become closely associated
with humanity, particularly in farmland areas where the combination of buildings like barns and byres for
nesting and livestock for providing fly-attracting poo make for a perfect lifestyle for the birds, and at good
spots they nest in loose colonies. People who play host to nesting Barn Swallows tend to become very fond of
'their' birds, look forward to their annual return in spring, mourn their departure in autumn, and are bereft if,
for whatever reason, the birds desert them entirely.

The journey

Barn Swallows usually produce two broods of chicks in a year, and those from the first brood, having nothing
in particular to do until migration time, may help their parents in rearing the second brood. By late summer
all those that have finished breeding will be spending their time feeding and flocking, often roosting in large
gatherings, sometimes with related species like Sand Martins (known in North America as Bank Swallows).
Roosts in reedbeds are quite common, giving rise to the old belief that swallows dived underwater to pass
winter bedded down in the mud, like some amphibians do. As the days shorten, swallows drift southwards
in flocks small and large, and may seem to loiter at the coast, going back and forth for some time before

striking out over the water. They prefer to cross land than sea, so in Europe large numbers reach Africa via Gibraltar or Italy.

The southbound migration for European birds is leisurely, with the birds taking every opportunity to pause, feed and drink on the way, particularly just prior to taking on the crossing of north Africa. At this time, the swallows lay down generous fat stores, particularly younger birds and particularly those on a route through Italy that will involve crossing the Mediterranean and then the widest part of the Sahara. (Those moving down through Iberia lay down significantly less fat.) Migrating in parties helps them to home in on good places to feed, although it does also attract predators. One in particular, the Eleonora's Falcon, which breeds on Mediterranean islands, times its breeding season so that it is feeding young in autumn, when the glut of migrating swallows and other small birds are passing through its breeding areas.

Once they have made it across the Sahara, the swallows continue south through more food-rich areas, although here they face the hazard of human hunters – large numbers are killed for food in Nigeria, Central African Republic and Congo. Some go on to the very southern tip of South Africa. Why do they go so far when acceptable conditions can be found much further north? Many western European songbirds make a much shorter journey, wintering just south of the Sahara, or even avoiding that dangerous crossing altogether and wintering in North Africa. Barn Swallows elsewhere also make what seem like excessively long migrations – in the Americas some migrate down to Tierra del Fuego, while eastern Asian birds may reach Australia. A Barn Swallow nesting in Europe and wintering in southern Africa flies more than 11,000km (6,835 miles) to reach its destination – 22,000km (13,670 miles) or more every year. Some North American Barn Swallows cover comparable distances.

If long-distance migration is not too challenging in itself for an animal, then going a bit further than you

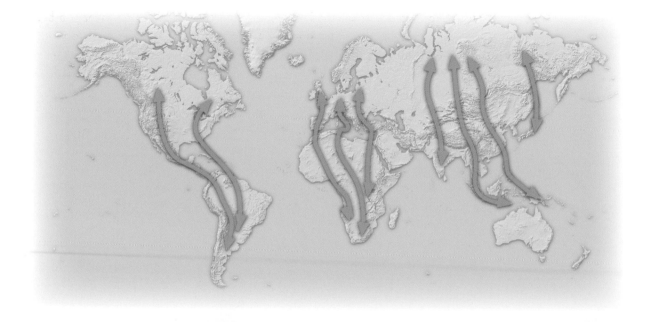

'have' to is a good move if it means that you'll have less competition for resources at your destination, and temperate regions will almost always offer a better deal than tropical areas. The fact that the Barn Swallow has colonised almost the whole world, when most other swallows have not spread beyond Africa, the continent where the swallow family is thought to have originated, indicates that it is a species for which serious journeying has become second nature.

As spring approaches, the swallows start to move northwards. They face the same dilemma as many other migrant birds – they want to reach the breeding grounds ahead of their rivals, to secure a good territory, but getting there too early is risky – temperate springs are unpredictable and early arrivals could be confronted by sub-zero nights and not enough flying insects to eat. Cold snaps in late spring can devastate swallow numbers – they are not versatile feeders and absolutely depend on good numbers of insects on the wing. This risk may even outweigh the various hazards they face while actually migrating. However, migration is shifting in accordance with climate change, with those wintering furthest south now setting off (and arriving) several days earlier, on average, than they did a few decades ago. Mean first arrival date in Guernsey, for example, was 8 April in 1903–1945, but 23 March in 1985–2005. This change shows the Barn Swallow's ability to adapt, but this can only go so far. Earlier arrival raises the risk of encountering inclement weather, and also cuts down the bird's 'off-duty' time in winter, when it is recovering from the rigours of breeding and migration.

Map: Barn Swallows around the world are long-distance migrants, taking the most direct overland route from Northern to Southern Hemisphere.

Arctic Tern

Sterna paradisaea

IUCN Least Concern

As our world is mostly sea, it makes sense that animals that live in the oceans – or are comfortable travelling over them – would be the most accomplished long-distance migrants. However, the bird that flies further than any other is not as effortless a seafarer than, say, the albatrosses – it is a small bird, weighing just 100g or so, with a rather frenetic-looking flight action, and it is not a good swimmer so cannot take a rest on the water's surface whenever it likes. All the more amazing, then, that the Arctic Tern flies up to 90,000km (55,925 miles) each year in its astounding pole-to-pole migration.

The traveller

Terns are seabirds that are closely related to gulls, but while gulls are mostly quite hefty and workman-like birds, terns are almost unbearably elegant. Because of their long, slim wings and deeply forked tails, some are known as 'sea swallows', and like swallows they are graceful and agile in flight. The Arctic Tern is a fairly typical example of tern-kind, a white-and-grey bird with a neat black cap, a pointed scarlet dagger for a bill, very long tail 'streamers', and dainty little feet that are not well-adapted for walking or (despite being webbed) swimming. It is a catcher of fish, crustaceans and other small marine animals but mainly achieves this by snapping them up at the water's surface while in flight – unlike some larger tern species it rarely dives and when it does its plunges are not very deep.

Arctic Terns nest in colonies at or near the coast in the Arctic and some northern temperate regions, on sea coasts, shingle islands in coastal rivers, and most abundantly on small islands that are free of mammalian predators such as Arctic Foxes. This bird is no pushover though, as any (human) visitor to a breeding colony will testify. At your approach, the terns rise up from their nests and launch their attack, diving at your head and doing their best to skewer your scalp with that extremely sharp bill – all the while keeping up an equally head-hurting racket of harsh rattling calls. The more terns in the colony, the more effective this is at seeing off predators, so Arctic Terns thrive and breed most successfully where they live in large and dense colonies. Other, less ferocious birds, such as phalaropes, often choose to nest at the edge of Arctic Tern colonies in order to benefit from the terns' hyper-vigilance. One hazard that never goes away is the attention of skuas (or jaegers) – gull-like birds that make their living by robbing other seabirds of the fish they catch. Arctic and Long-tailed Skuas (also known as Parasitic and Long-tailed Jaegers) are persistent tern-chasers and will continue to harass the terns during migration.

As is typical of seabirds, Arctic Terns are long-lived and with luck can survive well into their twenties or even mid-thirties. They do not begin breeding until three or four years old, and usually stick with the same mate for life, rearing one to three chicks each summer before the pair part for their epic journey to the other end of the earth. The bond between them is re-established when they return to their colonies the following spring, with courtship rituals including a high-flying display, aerial chases, and the solemn exchange of gifts of fish, all accompanied by much screeching.

These beautiful terns breed across the whole of the Arctic and parts of the sub-Arctic and their total global population is said by the IUCN to be about 2 million. Like many seabirds, they are vulnerable to the consequences of overfishing and marine pollution, and their low reproductive rate means they will not 'bounce back' quickly after a crash.

These graceful birds barely wet their feathers as they pluck fish from the sea surface.

The journey

Spending summer in the Arctic and winter at the Antarctic means that these birds experience two summers every year, albeit brief and not necessarily balmy ones, and see more daylight than any other animal. They travel at an average of 330km (205 miles) a day, but their migration is stop-start, with pauses at favourite staging areas to rest and feed. Although they need dry land (or floating objects) on which to roost, they can travel and forage well offshore, and prefer to stay in groups when travelling. On the Antarctic wintering grounds they rest on the pack-ice and on icebergs when not actively foraging.

The straight-line distance from breeding to wintering grounds is close to 20,000km (12,425 miles), so a round trip of 40,000km (24,850 miles) – a staggering distance for a smallish bird to fly in one year, in anyone's book. However, the actual route the birds take can be far longer. Use of tracking technology has revealed that some Arctic Terns cover well over double that distance. Researchers in Iceland and Greenland fitted geolocators to 11 adult, breeding Arctic Terns in the summer of 2011, and in 2012 were able to recapture all of their test subjects and retrieve the geolocators, and analyse the data gathered. The gadgets used are tiny devices, simpler and smaller than satellite tags that transmit real-time location data, but their capture of light level and temperature changes allows researchers to accurately plot exactly where the bird has been.

The study revealed that the birds did not all take the same route or reach the same end destination – some headed to the tip of South America and others went for southern Africa. The northbound route was long and meandering as the birds exploited prevailing winds, which carried them along at more than 500km (310 miles) a day in some cases. The tern that went furthest covered 81,600km (50,700 miles) on its round trip. In the lifetime of a veteran Arctic Tern, which can span 30 years or more, that amounts to more than 50 laps of planet Earth.

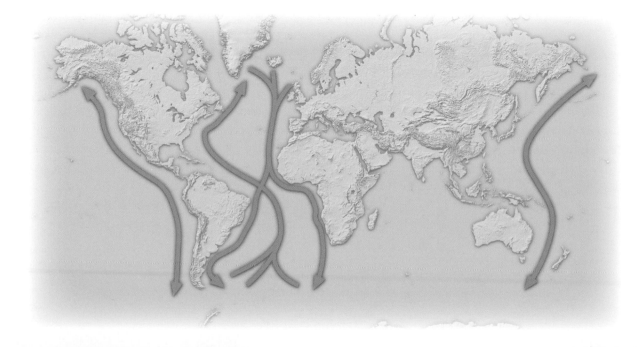

Another geolocator study over the same timespan produced even more startling results. These seven test subjects were caught on their nests in the Netherlands and all were recaptured the following year. Two of the seven had lost their geolocators somewhere en route but five sets of data were recovered. The Netherlands is at the southerly limit of the species' breeding range, so it might be supposed that these birds' journeys would be shorter. However, in fact the Dutch terns went even further, averaging 90,000km (55,925 miles) in their year of travel and going in a far from linear route. They visited the Atlantic, the central Indian Ocean and finally the Southern Ocean on their southbound route – one individual even went as far as New Zealand. The geolocators also revealed several staging areas which were hitherto unknown to science.

The vast distances covered by Arctic Terns on their migration underline the importance of cross-continental conservation efforts. They, along with other migrating terns, are hunted for food and sport in both South America and western Africa. However, it is when breeding that they are most vulnerable, and while the most northerly and remote colonies appear to be holding their own, further south they are declining. In a number of summers since 2000, British colonies have experienced near total breeding failure, with a shortage of the small fish they need for their chicks (especially sandeels) the likely cause. Climate change is another serious concern for this bird that spends much of its time at the two polar extremes.

Map: Tracking studies have shown that Arctic Terns may extend an already hugely long migration by taking indirect routes.

Above: In its inter-polar pursuit of endless daylight, the feisty Arctic Tern copes with snow and ice as well as sunshine.

Osprey

Pandion haliaetus

IUCN Least Concern

As the month of March nears its end, armchair birdwatchers around the world are eagerly checking and rechecking a webcam aimed at a double bed-sized birds' nest among the tall Scots Pines in Abernethy Forest, Scotland. Any day now, the stars of the show will arrive to begin their soap-opera summer of romance, conflict and parenthood. Many other long-established Osprey nests on both sides of the Atlantic are also now overseen by webcams, and the goings-on at each can be live-streamed into our homes. Watching Osprey family life 'as it happens' is enthralling enough, but now we can also follow what happens to them when summer ends and they set off on migration, thanks to the wonders of satellite-tracking.

A brood of three Osprey chicks close to fledging age
will need about four sizeable fish a day between them.

The traveller

The sole member of its taxonomic family, the Osprey is a special – and a specialised – bird of prey. It is one of very few birds that eats fish (and only fish) but does not dive, swim or even wade into the water. To be a land bird but to live on nothing but fish requires some notable anatomical adaptations, and some quite spectacular physical skill, and watching an Osprey circle over a shining lake, drop down and deftly pluck a big fish from the water with a smooth backward swipe of its talons is one of the most exhilarating experiences a wildlife-watcher can have.

At first glance, the Osprey resembles other large raptors, such as the buzzards, but has a more rangy shape with longer wings, and a more 'flappy', gull-like flight action. Its colour scheme is like that of many aerial fish-catchers – dark on the upperside but white on the underside, making it difficult to pick out when seen from below against a bright sky. It is distinguished by its long legs and big flexible feet, with fishhook claws and grippy rough skin on the soles of the toes, that help it hang onto its slippery prey. It can seal its nostrils for when it plunges into the water. Often only the feet break the surface and the Osprey can lift its prey clear without pausing in its arcing swoop. If it takes on a heavy fish it may be pulled down and momentarily immersed, but it has enough power to lift itself and its catch clear of the water.

Ospreys have a worldwide distribution, and those in the Northern Hemisphere are migrants, moving south when falling autumn temperatures encourage fish to stay in deeper water. Nest sites are in tall trees or on high structures, and are used year on year with more material added each time. Building a new nest is a major undertaking, as is forming a pair bond. Ospreys that have bred successfully are fiercely attached to 'their' nest, which is why they tend to pair with the same partner year after year as both head for the nest the moment they complete their spring migration – and Ospreys can live into their twenties, so it may be a long marriage, albeit one of convenience. A well-established pair will usually produce a clutch of three eggs, and in good years will successfully bring three chicks to fledging age, but it is common for the youngest chick to succumb to food shortages, as even in good years there are often lean spells as a result of spring storms that limit fishing opportunities for the adults. A weakened youngest chick is often helped on its way by brutal beatings from its older siblings, unwilling to compete for what food there is.

Young Ospreys do not normally return from the winter quarters until they are two or three years old, and it may then be several more years before they manage to breed. Many young Ospreys invest a great deal of time trying to displace the incumbent bird of their own sex from an established and successful nest, rather than setting up a home of their own, as finding a nest-site and building a big enough nest *and* finding a mate in time to breed is hugely demanding. Artificial nesting platforms are a big help for birds that don't yet have their own nest and have been instrumental in encouraging the species to spread and recolonise old haunts, as it bounces back from widespread declines over the early part of the 20th century.

The journey

Ospreys are early returners and late departers. In Britain, the first birds are back in late March, well before most of the small migratory songbirds, and they head straight for their nest, although they may then need to wander some distance to find a place where they can hunt. If there is unseasonably cold weather and lakes are frozen, they will go to the coast to fish.

In autumn, it is often the adult female of a nest who leaves first. The youngsters of the year go next, while the adult male hangs on until his last son or daughter has departed – only leaving when he is no longer needed to feed any hungry mouths. It may be a month or more between mother and father beginning their migration. It is thought that some young birds have not ever fished for themselves until they begin migration, and all will be inexperienced to say the least. With that skill to master, and a long migration to take on for the first time, it is hardly surprising that mortality in the first year is very high.

Most Ospreys from Britain spend their winters in west Africa, in Senegal and adjacent countries where there are fish-filled rivers offering good hunting all year round, although a few go no further than Spain. Tracking studies show that after reaching France they either hug the coast down to Spain or take a short-cut over the Bay of Biscay. Many do make a Sahara crossing rather than taking the coastal track to the final destination. Stop-offs are common and can be lengthy, with experienced birds having firm favourite points where they may spend weeks before resuming the journey. As you would expect, these birds with years of migration under their belt follow a much more predictable route than first-time youngsters, whose mistakes can prove fatal. One chick from Loch Garten headed west down the English Channel and never made it to land again, expiring in the mid-Atlantic 104 hours and 4,185km (2,600 miles) later. Another from the same nest went to the other extreme, making the record books when she completed her maiden 5,000km (3,100-mile) flight from Scotland to Senegal in just 14 days.

These birds' journeys were monitored via solar-powered satellite trackers, carried in the form of 'backpacks', which weigh 30g (about 2 per cent the weight of an adult Osprey). The trackers are set to transmit data at regular intervals, allowing for very detailed analysis of day-to-day movements. The batteries can survive for about three years, and the packs are designed to drop off the bird at around the same time. Sadly, most young birds tracked from Britain have not survived anywhere near this long – in most cases dying in Africa in their first winter rather than during the migration, from causes ranging from getting entangled in fishing net to collision with power cables. Predation is another factor, as west Africa is home to more and fiercer predators than Scotland. Some tracked adults from Scotland and Scandinavia, though, have sent valuable data for three years or more, and there are many active tracking studies ongoing in North America as well.

Tracking studies like these reveal an unprecedented level of detail about animal migration. They are also valuable tools for capturing human imagination, as they reveal something of the personalities of the individual birds they follow. There is nothing like this sense of personal connection to boost interest in conservation, and a general positive regard for Ospreys is one of the reasons the species is thriving and increasing around the world.

Map: Ospreys prefer to migrate overland but can cope with sea crossings better than most other large migratory birds of prey.

Above: Fitting Ospreys with rings (or bands) and satellite tags has helped us to understand their migratory movements.

Bar-tailed Godwit

Limosa lapponica

IUCN Near Threatened

Every country has its resident birds, and its summer and winter visitors. Most countries also have a fourth category of avian citizens – the passage migrants. Many of these are waders (or shorebirds, to give them their rather more apt North American moniker) of various kinds – breeding in the Arctic and heading far south for winter, but travelling slowly down the coasts of the countries in between and visiting many marshes and estuaries along the way in order to feed. One of these birds, though, has become famous not for a slow and steady, well-fed migration, but for making the longest non-stop flight of any bird, with not even a snack on the way.

The traveller

Godwits are large, elegant sandpipers with long legs and very long bills, which they use to poke soft mud and feel for invertebrates moving around within. They will also catch little fish in the shallows. All four species are devastatingly handsome in breeding plumage, with foxy-red tones setting off their intricate barred and dappled patterning. In winter they become much paler, greyer and drabber. Females are distinctly larger than males, but the roles of the sexes are more or less the same, with both parents looking after the chicks until they reach fledging age.

Bar-tailed Godwits breed north of the Arctic Circle across the whole of Eurasia and into Alaska. They are the smallest of the godwits – the western Eurasian subspecies being especially petite (for a godwit) – and are relatively short-legged, so look a little less catwalk model-like than the others in the group. Although they breed inland, on boggy and marshy tundra, they are coastal birds at all other times. On migration they usually stick to the sea shoreline itself, unlike the Black-tailed Godwit which favours coastal freshwater marshes – this habitat difference is one of the ways that birdwatchers in Europe can tell these two rather similar birds apart. In North America, the Bar-tailed Godwit rubs shoulders with the large and graceful Marbled Godwit, and the boldly patterned Hudsonian Godwit.

The journey

There are three subspecies of Bar-tailed Godwits in the world – the small form *lapponica*, breeding in Europe and western Asia; *menzbieri*, breeding in north-eastern Asia; and the largest form, *baueri*, breeding in far-eastern Asia and Alaska. All are migratory, but the one that goes the furthest is the subspecies *baueri*. This form migrates to Australia and New Zealand.

An old Maori story tells of how the ancestors of New Zealand's first people, setting out from eastern Polynesia over the sea in search of a new land, followed the flight path of the *kuaka* – the Bar-tailed Godwit. They could see by its long legs that the *kuaka* was a shorebird, not a seabird, so reasoned that when the birds came through on their south-eastern flight track, as they did each year, their destination must be dry land somewhere. They pointed their seagoing canoes in the same direction, and in due course discovered New Zealand, or Aotearoa – 'the land of the long white cloud'. Had they cared to look, they would also have found many *kuaka* feeding on the shorelines, regaining weight lost in a migratory flight of quite mind-bending proportions.

It was long known that the *baueri* godwits set out from Alaska in autumn and finish up in New Zealand, where they winter, and then reverse the process when heading back to the Arctic to breed in spring. The details of their route were not known but it seemed logical that, being shorebirds, they would make their way along coastlines, feeding on the way, as Bar-tailed Godwits further west were known to do. In 2006 and 2007, researchers caught a number of *baueri* godwits – some on the breeding grounds and others on the wintering grounds – and fitted them with satellite trackers. The data they received when the birds migrated showed that the migration route did not hug coastlines at all but instead crossed open ocean, for days on end. The birds had no opportunity to pause and feed, or even rest for a moment – they just flew, and flew, and flew.

Twenty-three birds were fitted with trackers in total – 12 females and 11 males. The females were fitted with surgically implanted trackers, while the males wore smaller externally mounted models. As mentioned before, female Bar-tailed Godwits are bigger than males, and the males were too light to carry the larger internal tracker. The surgically implanted model proved the more reliable, unsurprisingly – several of the males managed to lose their trackers but southbound migration was successfully tracked for seven females and two males. The godwit that flew the furthest was a female known as E7. This bird's southbound migration from Alaska to New Zealand took her 8.1 days, and covered 11,680km (7,258 miles). Four of the other tagged females covered more than 10,000 km – one of these took 9.4 days to complete her 10,026-km (6,230-mile) flight. The southbound migration of *baueri* Bar-tailed Godwits is by far the longest non-stop flight ever recorded for any species of bird, and is the longest journey without feeding that any animal on earth is known to make.

How does a godwit find its way over the featureless expanse of sea? This we do not know (yet) and can only speculate, based on what's known about animal navigation in general. At least some birds are known to

After breeding, the Bar-tailed Godwit moults into its drabber winter plumage, including a fresh set of flight feathers ready for migration.

use magnetite crystals in their bills to sense the Earth's magnetic field. They can also find their way through observing the changing positions of the stars and the sun. In the case of the godwits, the prevailing wind pushes them very much in the right direction.

Why the birds take on such an epic flight is probably to exploit these favourable winds, which save them a great deal of energy. Saving energy is another reason to make a non-stop flight. Bar-tailed Godwits fly at high altitudes when on their long-haul migration, at heights between 2,000–5,000m (6,600–16,400ft), and it would take a disproportionate amount of effort to regain that height after every pause. There is some evidence that the birds' metabolism shifts to a high-efficiency mode for migration, losing only 0.41 per cent of their body-weight per day – however, flight would be much less efficient if there were stop-offs to feed. Instead, they fuel up on a grand scale before they set off, laying down so much fat that they reach nearly double their post-migration weight. Another advantage of the sea crossing is avoiding predators – when on land, godwits may fall prey to eagles, large falcons and various other birds of prey, and also mammalian hunters, but when they are flying far out at sea there is nothing to threaten them except their own bodily limitations.

It is only the birds' southbound migration that takes the non-stop, oversea route. Those that were tracked heading north went the way that had been predicted at the start – following coastlines up through east Asia and making regular stop-offs. Prevailing winds are working against the birds now and doing the non-stop route in reverse, working against the winds, would presumably be too energetically costly and take too long for their fat reserves to last.

As of 2015, the Bar-tailed Godwit has been identified as a species of serious conservation concern, and the IUCN has placed it in the Near Threatened category. This is because of serious steep declines in the

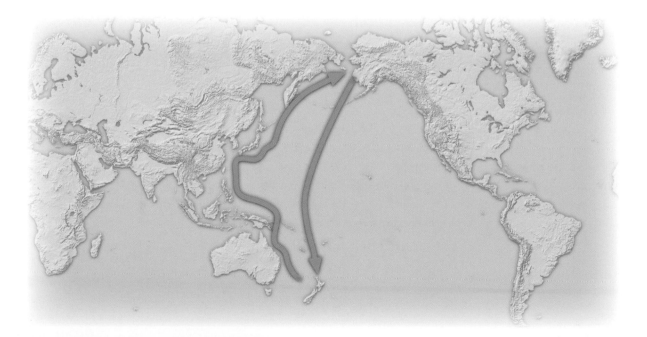

more easterly populations, including *baueri*. BirdLife International states that loss of suitable feeding habitat for migrants making their way along the east Asian coast is the key cause of the decline. Land reclamation, pollution and development are all seriously damaging vital stretches of muddy shoreline where the birds stop and feed on their northward migration. It is ironic that the Bar-tailed Godwit's record-breaking southbound journey, which has so dramatically redefined our understanding of migratory birds' powers of endurance, is now far safer than the much more mundane stop-start return journey.

Map: Far-eastern Bar-tailed Godwits heading south undertake the longest non-stop migration of any bird – as far as we know.

Above: Individually the Bar-tailed Godwit is a champion of endurance, but as a species its 'Near Threatened' status means that it is not currently one of life's winners.

Sooty Shearwater

Ardenna grisea

IUCN Near Threatened

Albatrosses lead quite an enviable life, if your idea of fun is spending most of your time traversing the endless oceans in (almost) effortless flight. Less well-known are the smaller cousins of the albatrosses, the shearwaters. These birds' small size imposes some restrictions on how and where they conduct the landbound part of their lives, when it's time to breed – they are much more vulnerable on land than are the big and burly albatrosses. However, they have the same torpedo-shaped, long-winged body plan that makes them so expert at long-distance flight at sea, and one of them in particular is better-travelled than any albatross.

The traveller

Shearwaters, albatrosses and petrels form an order of seabirds known as Procellariformes. This name is derived from the Latin word *procella* – a violent storm. This sums up these birds' ability to take on the wildest weather at sea, a skill that allows them to rack up some impressive mileage as they roam the oceans in search of food. There are nearly 30 species of shearwaters worldwide. They, along with various other similar seabirds, make up the family Procellariidae.

Unlike most birds, shearwaters and their relatives have a well-developed sense of smell, enhanced by their tubular nostrils (giving rise to another name for the group – 'tubenoses'). They can pick up the aroma of lunch from many kilometres away. The key smell is that of dimethylsulphide, a particularly pungent chemical produced when krill are feeding on plankton. The activity of the krill attracts other sea creatures, some of which are potentially food for the seabirds. Best of all is when large whales come to feed on the krill. They stir up the sea with their dives, bringing more prey to the surface for the birds – the whole effect is what's known as a 'food patch' and large numbers of shearwaters and other seabirds may congregate at such spots. Floating dead marine animals can also be important food sources for shearwaters, and they dive underwater to catch fish and squid. They are competent surface swimmers and can rest on the sea as needed.

The name 'shearwater' describes the way these birds fly – rising and falling, often dipping very close to the sea surface (photos reveal that their wingtips almost graze the water) and alternating fast flapping with lengthy, stiff-winged glides. They tilt from side to side as they go, so show their upper and undersides alternately – giving a particularly striking effect in those species that are dark above and white below. They keep energy expenditure down by using 'dynamic soaring' – making use of the changes in airspeed between the trough of a wave and its crest to help power their flight.

The Sooty Shearwater is a relatively large species, with dark blackish-brown plumage, but silvery linings to its underwings which flash on and off as the bird tips and tilts in its 'shearing' flight. It breeds on small islands in the south Pacific and south Atlantic oceans, with the highest numbers off southern Chile (especially Isla Guafo) and around New Zealand, where the dozens of colonies add up to about 5 million pairs. The total world population is in excess of 20 million individuals. Sooty Shearwaters and other small tubenoses nest in burrows, and arrive and leave their nests only at night, as they are awkward and slow on land and would be easy pickings for various predatory birds. They have always nested on islands that are free of mammalian predators, but ever since humans began to travel extensively by sea, their boats have helped the likes of rats and cats to find their way to such islands, where they can devastate shearwater colonies, by entering or reaching into burrows to kill incubating adults or chicks.

The journey

Sooty Shearwaters are regularly seen from the coast of Britain during migration periods, showing that they habitually make long migrations. As with other seabirds, getting a handle on exactly which route they take was always much more difficult than with landbirds, whose progress may be directly observed over much of their route, and understood in more detail through recoveries and retrappings of ringed birds. Trapping and ringing seabirds is really only feasible at their breeding colonies – retrapping a living ringed bird when it is away from the breeding ground is highly improbable. Some ringed birds may be recovered when their remains are washed up on shore, but they are few and far between, and such data is of limited use anyway as there is no way to be sure how far their corpses were carried by the sea after their deaths.

Today, though, tracking technology allows us to follow the journeys of birds like the Sooty Shearwater, and often reveals that whatever we might have guessed about the distance of their migrations falls far short of the reality. A study spanning 2005 to 2006 involved researchers fitting geolocators to a total of 33 Sooty Shearwaters, all adult birds breeding on islands around New Zealand. The trackers were set to record position, ambient temperature and dive depth, so would provide full details of the routes taken by the birds, and the dive depth figures would allow the researchers to infer detail about the birds' feeding behaviour on the journey. Twenty of these birds were recaptured at their burrows the following breeding season, and 19 of the recovered geolocators yielded temperature and position data while 11 of those 19 also produced dive depth data.

The tracked birds were found to describe a huge figure-of-eight loop across the whole Pacific Ocean, spending the austral winter at one of three 'hot-spots' (off Japan, Alaska or California) before looping back again, apparently making the most of trade winds in both directions. The total flight covered up to 65,000km (40,400 miles) – the longest animal migration known, until recent research on Arctic Terns showed that they

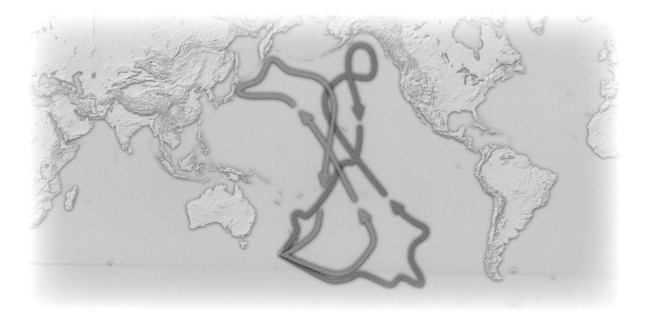

go even further. The trip was entirely offshore, well away from the land with all its dangers for these most pelagic birds.

The shearwaters travelled at high speed, from 724–1,096km (450–680 miles) a day. They did not travel in flocks, though congregations at good feeding spots occurred naturally. On their return route they showed surprising synchronicity, all passing through the same narrow corridor and crossing the Equator within a 10-day window in October. The dive depth figures showed that these birds, built for flight rather than swimming, were nonetheless able to reach impressive depths of up to 68m (223ft), although the average was just 14m (46ft). Interestingly, there seemed to be no correlation between the birds' natal colony and where they spent the winter.

A willingness and ability to travel long distances to find the best places to feed is evident in Sooty Shearwater breeding behaviour as well. When feeding young, parents may disappear for as long as 15 days, heading down to the Antarctic polar front where rich fishing grounds are to be found, away from competition with other, less adventurous fish-eating seabirds. The chicks are well adapted to lengthy fasts, with the promise of a huge meal of regurgitated fish and squid on each parent's return. Young Sooties are much heavier than adults when close to fledging.

Although still staggeringly numerous, this seabird is declining quickly enough that the IUCN has classed it as Near Threatened. The dangers it faces include predation by rats at some breeding sites – rats are very capable of completely exterminating colonies if left unchecked. A large number of fat well-grown chicks ('muttonbirds') are harvested for food by human hunters across the breeding range, although probably not enough to explain the current decline. Hazards at sea include being accidentally caught in driftnets or snagged on longline fishing hooks – although both of these are being addressed by legislation. However, climate change could be a key driver of the decline, affecting the productivity of traditional foraging areas. The Sooty Shearwater's ability to adapt to this change may soon be severely tested.

Map: The complex figure of eight route followed by Sooty Shearwaters outside the breeding season is guided by food availability and prevailing winds.

Above: Sooty Shearwaters often travel in flocks, taking their cues from each other when it comes to finding food.

Wilson's Storm-Petrel

Oceanites oceanicus

IUCN Least Concern

Setting sail from southern and south-west England, passenger ferries bound for Santander and Bilbao cross the Bay of Biscay, the vast deep gulf of the north Atlantic that fits into the curved waist of coastline formed by western France and northern Spain. While many of those aboard will be holidaymakers keen to try the pool, relax on the sun-deck and sample every dish on offer at the buffet, others will be more interested in scanning the seas from dawn until dusk, looking out for signs of ocean life. Here is a great opportunity to see the giants of the seas – Fin Whale, the second largest animal to have ever lived, is regularly seen in good numbers on the crossings, along with many other species of whales and dolphins, some of them great rarities. Those with an interest in birds, though, will be trying to get their eye in on something much smaller – a tiny and incredibly delicate-looking seabird, but one with big ambitions for world travel.

Like all petrels, Wilson's Storm-Petrel has tubular nostrils to accentuate its well-developed sense of smell.

The traveller

With a name like *Oceanites oceanicus*, it is clear that Wilson's Storm-Petrel is acknowledged to be a true seabird. However, it and the other storm-petrels look, at first glance, quite ill-equipped for life on the ocean waves. They are very small for a start, barely bigger than a sparrow, with broad rounded wings that flutter, rather than the long, narrow and blade-like gliding wings of birds like shearwaters and albatrosses. When foraging, they have the engaging habit of dangling down their long, slender legs and 'pattering' their little webbed feet on the surface of the water. It is this behaviour which led to their being called 'petrels' – after St Peter, who is said to have walked on water.

Appearances are often deceptive in the natural world, and these dainty little birds actually belong to the same order as the shearwaters and albatrosses – Procellariiformes. Their family is Hydrobatidae, a sister group to the larger tubenoses. They share with their big cousins an ability to roam the seas for months on end and to locate food by smell, and they are also incredibly long-lived for their size, provided they manage to steer clear of the many predators that would find them a convenient little mouthful. With good fortune they stand a chance of living into their thirties, much longer than similar-sized landbirds. There is some evidence that they have unusual chromosomes – the telomeres at the ends of each chromosome lengthen rather than shorten (as is known to happen in most other organisms) with age, potentially protecting the chromosome from age-related deterioration over time. The phenomenon of lengthening telomeres has been confirmed in one species (Leach's Storm-Petrel) and is likely to be present in other storm-petrels too. It is likely to be the key to their unusually long lifespan.

Wilson's Storm-Petrel looks very like the European Storm-Petrel of the Northern Hemisphere – a small-billed, long-legged dark blackish-brown seabird with a large white rump patch. Birdwatchers seeking Wilson's from British waters need a good look to differentiate the two species. However, Wilson's is a Southern-Hemisphere breeder, like the Sooty Shearwater. It nests on the Antarctic coastline and on many adjacent islands, nesting in the gaps and crevices in boulder scree.

As with other tubenoses, it has a low reproductive rate, producing just one chick per year, and not breeding until at least three years old. The parents show extreme loyalty to their nest-site and to each other, even though they spend the austral winter wandering the seas alone. Like other small tubenoses, Wilson's Storm-Petrel visits its nest at night to evade predatory birds like skuas (jaegers) and gulls. It cannot cope at all with mammalian predators that could access its nests, and the accidental introduction of rats to an island could result in the loss of a whole colony. However, most breed further south than such predators could survive.

Wilson's Storm-Petrel is the smallest endothermic ('warm-blooded') animal that breeds in Antarctica. Its ability to endure the hardships of polar life carry a great reward. It has very little in the way of competition for the resources it needs, and so it is one of the most abundant bird species in the world with a population

Overleaf: The austere beauty of the South Shetland
Islands – one of many Southern Hemisphere
breeding grounds for Wilson's Storm-Petrel.

of more than 12 million individuals, perhaps as many as 30 million. Outside of the breeding season, those many millions of tiny petrels spend their lives wandering far out at sea and only a small proportion of them are ever seen by human eyes.

The journey

After breeding, Wilson's Storm-petrels migrate north and cross the equator. They may cover 10,000km (6,215 miles) or more, although the details of routes taken are not yet known and are likely to show much individual variation. Most spend the winter in the north Atlantic or north Indian Ocean, while some winter in the Pacific. This is the only storm-petrel to regularly undertake such long-distance migrations. Not very many Wilson's go a long way north but enough do that birdwatchers regularly see them from pelagic trips around the UK's Isles of Scilly in autumn, and they have been recorded as far north as Svalbard and Alaska. The best areas to see them are along the continental shelf, where upwellings of very deep water provide lots of suitable food at the sea surface.

Living away from land for months at a time requires certain adaptations. Like other tubenoses, Wilson's Storm-Petrels can locate food or areas of general feeding activity by smell. This fact is exploited on wildlife-watching boats, where 'chum' (a stinking concoction of fish scraps, guts and oil) is thrown onto the sea to

attract them. When not following boats, the petrels will feed on plankton but also relish the floating excreta of whales. Water needs are met by drinking seawater – along with many other seabirds, all petrels have salt glands that allow them to filter excess salt from the water they drink and excrete it through the nostrils in the form of salty water droplets, disposed of with a quick head-shake.

These small birds are not quick or powerful fliers but they can handle stormy weather, up to a point. However, they can occasionally get into difficulties and end up inland, although in Europe at least it is the related Leach's Storm-Petrel that is much more prone to turning up on rivers and reservoirs after gales at sea. However, in South America, inland records of Wilson's Storm-petrel are frequent enough to have led to the suggestion that they may migrate overland deliberately. There are regular records of birds in the Argentine Andes, up to 120km (75 miles) inland and sometimes even in small flocks. For this species, traversing land is potentially as hazardous as crossing the sea is for small landbirds, offering no opportunity to rest or feed. It is also possible that there is an as yet undiscovered inland-nesting population of Wilson's Storm-petrels. For such an abundant little bird, this species remains highly enigmatic, although as satellite tracking technology advances, we are likely to greatly expand our understanding of all storm-petrels' behaviour at sea over the coming years.

Map: Perhaps following no particular path, these little petrels wander across more than half of the world's 'sea-space' after the breeding season.

Above: Despite their delicate appearance, these petrels are seriously tough long-distance travellers.

Ruby-throated Hummingbird

Archilochus colubris

IUCN Least Concern

In every sense of the word, hummingbirds dazzle. Their powers of flight are the stuff of legend, although more so for pin-point precise manoeuvres in small spaces than for long-distance travel. However, the hummingbirds' family tree reveals that their closest relatives *are* a group of renowned long-haul fliers – the swifts. Hummingbirds for the most part are not migrants – most species live in the tropics and their travels are limited to moving up or down the hillsides as they follow the flowering cycles of various plants. Those species that breed further north, though, are true migrants.

The male Ruby-throated Hummingbird is a glittering gem.

The traveller

Found only in the Americas, the hummingbirds are specialist nectar-feeders and have evolved an incredibly flexible wing anatomy and agile flight mode that allows them to hover on the spot or make minute adjustments through three dimensions while feeding – no other bird can fly backwards.

Their fast-thrumming wings (on average 50 beats a second) produce a definite hum as they move from flower to flower, lapping up the high-octane fuel they need to sustain that level of energy output. Males of some species have a loud signature 'trill', produced by the vibration of particular wing and/or tail feathers, which functions to signal their sex and proclaim their territory to potential mates and to rivals. As well as hanging on the spot, hummingbirds can unleash a tremendous turn of speed, most often observed when seeing off a rival from 'their' clump of blossoms. All this frantic calorie-burning ends abruptly at night, when their metabolic rate can plummet as they enter a state of torpor, with body temperature falling from 40°C (104°F) to 18°C (64°F), and heart rate slowing from more than 1,000 beats per minute to just 50–180 – without this adaptation they would struggle to survive the hours of darkness without feeding.

Compared to Central and South America, the USA has rather few species of hummingbirds on its national list – about 23, out of a grand total of some 330–340 species in the whole family. About six of these are rare visitors or vagrants, and most of the rest are known only from the most southerly states. Naturally, the people of the USA are proud of their little gang of tough-cookie hummingbirds and put out food for them in the form of sugar-water, which is dispensed from special feeders. Even people living in large cities can attract hummingbirds this way – the feeders can be suctioned to an apartment window and provide wonderful close-up views of one of the true marvels of nature. These feeding stations can also be a real life-line to hummers that are about to begin migration, or have just completed it.

For a bird whose weight rarely exceeds 4g, the Ruby-throated Hummingbird is a particularly tough cookie. It is a solitary bird and a territorial one, only putting up with others of its kind at the start of the breeding season when males allow females into their territories for mating. After this, the female is on her own – she builds a tiny cup of a nest, lays two eggs in it, and incubates them alone. The chicks are fed bill-to-bill on regurgitated nectar, which their mother can deliver to them while hovering, such is her sublime aerial skill. After three weeks in the nest, the chicks fledge. At this age they look like their mother – greyish above and whitish below with an emerald-green sheen when the light strikes them just so.

As they mature the young males gradually develop the shining red throat patch that gives the species its name. This area of colour is broad and vivid on fully mature males, and has a definite scaled appearance. Like the green on the back, it is iridescent and its apparent shade changes with the angle of light, from pink to scarlet to violet. Females are a little larger than males, and ringing recovery data shows that they also live longer. It is thought that the males may 'burn themselves out' through the vigour of their territorial defence.

The journey

The two most widespread species of hummingbirds are the Ruby-throated and the Rufous Hummingbirds, both of which are found across much of the USA and even reach Canada. Both are long-distance migrants, and while the Rufous makes a longer journey – up to 3,200km (1,990 miles) each autumn, and the same again on the return trip in spring from its wintering grounds in Mexico – the Ruby-throated's autumn migration to Mexico, Central America or the West Indies can reach 3,000km (1,860 miles) or so and is arguably more challenging, as its route is not just overland but involves crossing the Gulf of Mexico. This 800km (500-mile) flight over water must be accomplished all in one go.

This is a huge challenge for such a small bird, whose tiny body is such a relentlessly demanding energy furnace. No wonder people formerly believed that hummers migrated by hitching a ride on the backs of bigger, more robust migratory birds. A hummingbird in flight has a higher metabolic rate than any other animal – its oxygen consumption is 10 times higher than that of an elite human athlete putting in maximal effort. Scale up the hummingbird to human size and it would need to consume 155,000 calories a day to sustain its energy output. That a Ruby-throated Hummingbird can complete a 20-hour non-stop flight without taking fuel on board en route seems impossible, but it is aided by the prevailing winds, and straight-line flight is less demanding than hovering flight. Pre-migration, a Ruby-throat fuels up enough to double its body-fat reserves, and every last milligram of that fat is then burned up in the Gulf crossing.

The Ruby-throat is a wonderful example of a migrant that pushes all boundaries to make its way of life a success. It cannot afford any mistakes on this stage of its migration, and once it completes the overnight sea crossing it must feed straight away to power up its batteries. The overland parts of migration are less risky. Migrating hummingbirds fly low most of the time – they have not been observed at heights above about 150m (500ft). They can therefore stop to feed whenever they choose, and can rest at night. There are

observations of them flying very low over the sea as well, and even apparently using the crests of waves as windbreaks. On northbound migration in spring, the route is entirely overland – a longer trip, but the Gulf crossing is not an option for them without the prevailing wind in their favour. It has been shown that birds heading north follow the 1.7°C (35°F) isotherm (night temperature) as it progresses, so they avoid freezing night-times by the slimmest of margins. As ever, the dilemma is to arrive in breeding areas early enough to secure a good territory but late enough for the weather to be survivable, but the margin for error is as tiny as the hummingbirds themselves.

Climate change appears to be affecting the migratory route of the Rufous Hummingbird, with increasing numbers moving eastwards on their south-bound journey, and wintering in the far south-eastern US states rather than sticking to the west of the continent and wintering in western Mexico. For Ruby-throats, which work so close to their own physical limits as well as the seasonal shifts in their environment, climate change could have even more significant consequences. At present, though, the species is increasing, no doubt helped greatly by an army of hummingbird enthusiasts up and down the USA, and the series of amply stocked 'roadside cafés' they provide for the migrating birds.

Map: The southbound route of the Ruby-throated Hummingbird involves significant (though wind-assisted) sea crossings. Returning birds take a longer, overland route.

Above: Female Ruby-throated Hummingbirds are less colourful than their mates but every bit as beautiful.

Bohemian Waxwing

Bombycilla garrulus

IUCN Least Concern

At the time of writing, winter in Britain is coming to an end, and it has not been a 'waxwing winter'. The winters of 2010–2011 and 2012–2013 were very different, and from mid-autumn, thousands of these lovely punk-crested birds pitched up along the east coast and spread rapidly inland – a ravenous army intent on eating every last berry from every single tree. The Bohemian Waxwing is not a true long-distance migrant in that its more extreme movements are unpredictable. This is a response to the availability of the food it eats in winter, and for birdwatchers this makes it a particularly exciting and enigmatic species.

Waxwings in winter are highly social and not at all shy.

The traveller

There are three species of waxwings in the world, distributed around the Northern Hemisphere. The Cedar Waxwing is in North America, the Japanese Waxwing in east Asia, and the Bohemian Waxwing fills the gap and occupies northern Europe and north-west Asia, but also shares the turf of the other two species, being found across north-east Asia and in North America too. The three are very similar-looking, being sleek, chunky starling-sized birds with pinky-orange plumage, a black mask and chin, and further accessorised with patches of black, red and yellow on the wings and tail. Their crowning glory is a long, soft crest, giving a distinctive outline when all you see (as is often the case) is a group of silhouettes in a tree-top. The Bohemian Waxwing is the biggest and most colourful of the waxwings, and its breeding range is very northerly – mainly 60–67°N.

This bird is a frugivore – a fruit-eater. When breeding it takes some insects too, and the chicks need that boost of protein, but adults in winter eat virtually nothing but fruit – mainly berries but also larger fruit such as apples when berries are hard to find. Fruits are full of sugar but rather lacking in other nutrients, so must be eaten in large quantities. In winter, Bohemian Waxwings are highly gregarious, with flocks searching for decent stands of fruiting trees. They converse constantly as they move around, a charming rolling trill of a call that could be likened to festive sleigh-bells. Berries are plucked and swallowed whole at a prodigious rate, while the birds' colourful berry-stained poo rains down from the trees – a flock of feeding waxwings is a delightful sight but you don't want to park your car underneath them!

This sociality is not even suspended during the breeding season – pairs will nest close to each other and there is little territorial aggression, just minor skirmishes over prime nesting spots. The incubating female receives food from her mate in the form of regurgitated fruit, and he brings insects for the chicks while they are small. As the chicks grow, and become sufficiently developed to maintain their own body heat without being brooded, the female joins the male in fetching food, which switches from insects to fruit. By the time they fly, the chicks are ready to begin their own career of berry-stripping.

Overleaf: The extensive boreal forests of the Northern Hemisphere provide breeding habitat for Bohemian Waxwings.

The journey

In most years, Bohemian Waxwings make relatively short movements southwards to escape the severe sub-Arctic winter and to find the food they need. However, every year for these birds is different. Because of its restricted diet, the Bohemian Waxwing faces a problem – in some years, fruiting trees don't do very well and the berry crop is sparse. The birds move south in any case when winter arrives, but if they can't find enough food they have to just keep on moving. In the case of the northern European breeders, this means heading south and west. In years when the berry crop fails completely in their usual winter range, they undertake a mass long-distance movement – what's known as an irruption. This happens across their whole range, and Cedar and Japanese Waxwings are also irruptive.

Birdwatchers often suppose that irruptive movements are in response to bad weather. When great numbers of hungry Bohemian Waxwings started to arrive in Shetland, Orkney and north-east Scotland in October 2010, there was widespread conviction that a severe winter was heading our way. As it turned out, this was exactly what happened – there was heavy snow for the north in November and for the rest of the country through December, in one of the most dramatically snowy British winters in living memory. However, waxwing irruptions are just as likely in mild winters – there was another big waxwing arrival in the meteorologically unremarkable winter of 2012–13. Snow and cold is no hardship for these birds as long as they have enough to eat. It really is all about the berries.

The same goes for other irruptive bird species, although the foodstuff involved may be different. In late summer and autumn 2013, there was an irruption of crossbills into Britain, with three different species involved including the rare Two-barred Crossbill, which rarely ventures into western Europe – crossbills specialise in eating pine seeds, and their movements are dictated by the success or failure of the pine crop. In 2015–16, it was the turn of Short-eared Owls to show up en masse in Britain. These owls are specialist vole-hunters, and in Europe they make short-range or long-distance movements in search of good numbers of Short-tailed Voles.

Left: With their striking looks, Bohemian Waxwings are much loved by birdwatchers.

Issues with finding food are compounded by the number of birds that are searching. The 'perfect storm' conditions for an irruption occur when a very successful breeding season is followed by a lack of autumn or winter food. The 2010–11 Bohemian Waxwing arrival involved a high proportion of juvenile birds, suggesting there had been good conditions for breeding that summer.

For birdwatchers and especially bird photographers, meeting a flock of Bohemian Waxwings is a total delight. The birds are very beautiful, full of energy and often extremely approachable – the first arrivals in Shetland in 2010 were even photographed coming to people's hands to eat apples. But for the birds, irruption is not a joy at all – it is a last-ditch bid to survive when times have become very tough. Waxwings are not especially built for travel – they are built to endure cold, with their dense soft plumage and stocky shape, but their diet doesn't allow them to easily lay down extra fat stores to survive lengthy flights. And in any case it is a shortage of food that drives them to move, so they may already be running on empty. They may also make life difficult for other birds such as Robins and thrushes, which also depend quite heavily on winter berry crops.

Irruptions are a natural part of life for birds like waxwings. Many will starve in irruption years, but those that do make it through and survive the journey back north are likely to have breeding success the following spring, with less competition for food and nest-sites. Of course, that will seem a long way off to a flock of starving birds roaming an unfamiliar land in desperate search of food.

One point in their favour, though, is the increasing trend to brighten up shopping centres, service stations and other urban eyesores by planting attractive berry-bearing trees such as rowans, and shrubs like pyracantha and cotoneaster, in the open areas. These concentrations of fruiting trees can be true life-savers for hungry waxwings. If garden space allows, it's worth planting a few yourself – you could then enjoy a visitation from these beautiful northern nomads the next time they invade.

Map: Bohemian Waxwings travel variable distances – south-west in Eurasia, or south-east in North America – in order to find food in winter.

Blackcap

Sylvia atricapilla

IUCN Least Concern

A number of western European songbirds, including the Blackcap and nearly all of its fellow warblers, migrate a relatively short distance south to spend winter in northern Africa. A migration of somewhere between 2,000–3,000km (1,240–1,860 miles) doesn't seem all that impressive, especially when compared to the likes of Barn Swallow with its 11,000km (6,850-mile) trip to the southern tip of Africa. What's interesting about the Blackcap is not the length or route of its migration as such, but the fact that its migratory habits are changing, and changing quickly and dramatically. We are in the privileged position of being able to observe, monitor and study this as it happens.

The traveller

Blackcaps are early returners to western Europe, and by the end of March most keen birdwatchers in the southern half of Britain will have heard a male or two singing. This is a common bird of deciduous woodland and parkland, liking a mix of mature trees and dense undergrowth. It is rather shy and retiring, staying in cover most of the time, and is easier to hear than see. The male's song is very tuneful and fluty, with a rich quality that recalls larger songsters like the Common Blackbird. So celebrated is its song that it is sometimes known locally as the 'northern nightingale' – as it occurs further north in Britain than the much scarcer real Nightingale. It is widespread across Europe and western Asia.

Unlike most warblers, this is a sexually dimorphic species, easily assigned to male or female by the colour of its cap – black in males, warm brown in females. The rest of the plumage is soft grey, darker on the upperside than the underside. It is a slim and elegant bird which mainly forages in the trees, and eats insects, switching more to berries and other fruit in early autumn before it begins its migration. It produces one brood per year (sometimes two in the south of its range), of four to six young, and the chicks resemble rather drab versions of their mother on fledging but the young males acquire black caps in their post-juvenile moult, before migration. Rather unusually, Blackcaps defend their territories not just against other Blackcaps, but against the closely related, and vocally extremely similar, Garden Warbler as well.

The journey

Ringing recoveries have shown that the Blackcaps that breed in Britain head for Iberia and north Africa in winter. If you happen to be in southern Spain in January you'll see this for yourself – Blackcaps are very, very common (and much less so in the breeding season). Back in Britain, the only warbler you would see in winter, up until the 1960s, was the Dartford Warbler, a long-tailed little sprite

Only the adult male Blackcap has a black crown –
females and young birds have a chestnut-brown cap.

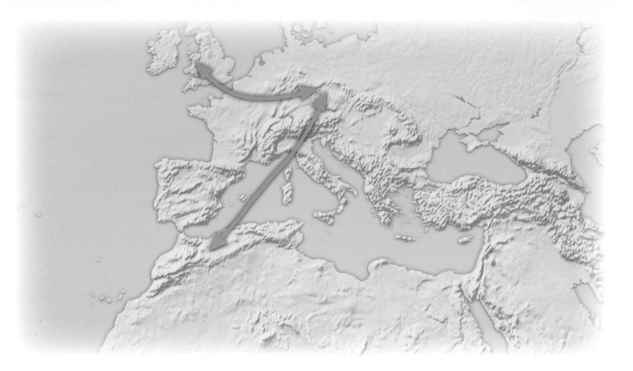

of lowland heath. The garden bird table was the domain of tits and finches, who would bicker over peanuts and kitchen scraps.

However, from the 1970s, there was a new kid on the block, and it was making its presence very much felt. Tyrannising the tits and getting into fisticuffs with the finches, this new arrival was a real brawler. Many casual back-garden watchers didn't recognise it, never having seen one in spring or summer. These overwintering Blackcaps seemed to have had complete personality transplants – not only had they failed to migrate, but they scrapped fiercely for food and were not even worried by human observers.

Over the last part of the 20th century, the numbers of Blackcaps overwintering in Britain increased dramatically, and their distribution also spread northwards. For many birdwatchers it was soon easier to see a Blackcap in winter than in summer, although numbers in summer were actually increasing through that period (and still are today). Individual Blackcaps in winter seem to hold territory in a garden or gardens for many weeks at a time – sometimes a pair would be present but otherwise they were intolerant of other Blackcaps, as well as most other garden birds. Even the famously fierce Robin often took a beating from a Blackcap, especially when a favourite food such as a block of fat was on offer.

It was presumed, naturally enough, that these Blackcaps were British breeding birds that had, for whatever reason, not migrated. However, ringing recoveries revealed that they were not – in fact they were from further east in Europe, mainly birds which had bred in Germany. Previous data from ringing reports said that German Blackcaps, just like British ones, migrated to Iberia and north Africa – but it was clear that a growing proportion of them had made a switch and now headed west rather than south and south-west.

Time for some serious science. Scientists used captive German-bred Blackcaps to investigate two things

The map shows the two different migratory
routes taken by eastern European Blackcaps.

BLACKCAP

– the behaviour of the birds at migration time, and whether genetics could explain the change in behaviour. It was found that the birds showed a tendency to orient themselves either west or south when autumn approached, indicating which direction they 'wanted' to migrate. Cross-breeding studies showed that the migratory behaviour bred true – with west-preferring pairs producing only west-preferring young, and the same for the birds which preferred moving south. This suggested that a very simple genetic difference separated the two groups – perhaps just a single point mutation (a change to only one gene) – the sort of change that could arise in one generation. Clearly if British-born Blackcaps carried a new genetic mutation that would make them migrate west instead of south, that mutation would not be passed on to the next generation, because the Blackcaps would fly out over Ireland and then the open Atlantic on their first migration, and that would be their last migration. Very few passerines have ever managed to reach North America from Europe (prevailing winds mean more have made the crossing the other way around). But the German-born birds that migrated westwards got lucky, and when their brains told them they had completed their journey, they were in Britain – land of free food if you could find a garden with a well-stocked bird table. So those carrying the new mutation survived, and passed it on to their offspring.

From one little random mutation, a whole world of difference has opened up between the 'westies' and the 'southies'. They share the same habitats in the same countries in summer, but their winter lifestyles are quite different, and natural selection is beginning to modify the 'westies' in ways that better suit their lifestyle. They have a slightly shorter migration than the 'southies' but have to survive lower temperatures – they also have different diets. The two groups are beginning to diverge accordingly, 'westies' becoming shorter-winged, browner and slimmer-billed.

What happens when the two different groups come back together in Germany and prepare to breed? Isotope analysis of breeding pairs has shown that they stick to their own 'kind' – mainly because the shorter-migrating 'westies' are all back on territory before the 'southies' return. This also means that the 'westies' secure better nest-sites than 'southies' and so are likely to have better breeding success.

This little bird has provided us with a real-life experiment into how a small, genetically caused change in migration habits can turn one population of an animal into two, and perhaps in due course the two 'types' will even become fully separate species. There are other species which appear to be showing a similar change – for example, a few Pallas's and Yellow-browed Warblers from Siberia now migrating west rather than south, and surviving winter and returning to Siberia to breed the following spring. However, their numbers are tiny compared to the 'westie' Blackcaps and their storming takeover of Britain's winter gardens. However, it will all come crashing down for the pioneer Blackcaps if they cannot continue to rely on garden birdfeeders as their main source of winter food – it is a grand evolutionary change built entirely on the rather fragile foundation of human goodwill.

Leatherback Turtle

Dermochelys coriacea

IUCN Vulnerable

Huge and heavy though they are, the marine turtles are quite breathtakingly graceful in motion underwater, seeming to fly along with smooth strokes of their long, flattened, flipper-like forelimbs. When you consider that their land-dwelling relatives, the tortoises, are living representations of ponderous slowness, this is all the more remarkable. Among reptiles, most species are terrestrial, although there are Marine Iguanas and various sea-snakes, and some crocodilians are semi-marine. However, the sea turtles are by far the most well-adapted to life in the sea, and accordingly are the wide-ranging reptiles geographically, although they remain tied to the land for breeding purposes. As a group, the sea turtles are in serious trouble and observing them today is a privilege that future generations may be denied. Of the seven described species, six are considered to be of conservation concern, while the seventh is not yet well known enough to have a conservation status.

Slow and awkward on land, the Leatherback becomes
a vision of effortless grace when it takes to the sea.

The traveller

The world's sea turtles fall into two families – the Leatherback in a family of its own (Dermochelyidae) and the other six making up the family Cheloniidae. The Leatherback is the biggest of them, among reptiles only being out-sized by three species of hefty crocodile. It is distinguished by its fleshy-looking carapace, which has a layer of skin on top rather than being bare and hard. The broad, fairly flat back bears seven longitudinal ridges. Compared to the other sea turtles, it is more streamlined, with a tear-drop shape. Fully grown, it can be nearly 3m (10ft) long and 1.5m (5ft) across, and can weigh close to 700kg (1,545lb). Its front flippers are nearly as long as its whole body, and are proportionately longer than those of other sea turtles.

Sea turtles famously 'nest' on particular beaches, with each female returning to the same beach regularly (though not necessarily every year) to lay her eggs, after mating in the sea close by. She buries her eggs in the sand and then lumbers back into the sea, leaving the eggs to their fate. The hatchlings have to dig their way out and then rush to the sea, dodging the many opportunistic predators that come to feast on them. They are still vulnerable once in the water, being very small, but they can at least move much more freely and quickly, the way nature intended. As they grow, their chances of being predated shrink, and few animals in the sea or on the land would even think about tackling a full-grown sea turtle of any species. As long as they make it to adulthood, they are likely to live into their forties or fifties.

Leatherbacks nest around Central America, West Africa and Indonesia, in two main population groups. A Leatherback female lays up to nine clutches through the breeding season, each comprising about 110 eggs. She digs out a nest on a beach of soft sand below an area of forest, above the high-water mark. She picks a moonlit night to help her find her way (vision out of water is very poor) and orients herself towards the dark of the forest to find the right part of the beach, and then when the laying is complete she heads for the brightness of the moonlit sea. Occasionally, a Jaguar kills an egg-laying Leatherback, but it is the eggs and young that are particularly vulnerable. Some human communities have a long tradition of digging up turtle eggs for consumption, although many important beaches are now protected. Left alone, the eggs hatch one night after about 60–70 days – the surrounding temperature determines whether the young develop as male or female, with more females hatching from warmer sand.

The male hatchlings, if they make it to the sea, will never leave it again, while females will begin their beach visits to lay eggs once they reach breeding age (probably about 9–15 years old). When not assembling near nesting beaches to mate, these turtles will spend the next few decades roaming the oceans to find good concentrations of jellyfish, their primary food source. They will dive to depths of 1,000m (3,280ft) in search of food – deeper than any other air-breathing animal except a few species of whales – and can tolerate near-freezing water, meaning that they are able to travel through virtually every stretch of ocean on Earth.

The journey

In a sense, Leatherback migration begins from the moment the finger-long hatchling busts out of its egg. It must orient itself towards the sea and get there as quickly as it can. Moonlight shining on the sea is what guides it the correct way, just as it was for its mother a couple of months before. For this reason, artificial lighting near nesting beaches can have a harmful effect as it can draw the young turtles the wrong way.

It has been shown experimentally in some other sea turtles that they swim perpendicular to wave crests, a strategy that will take them out to sea. Once well away from the shore they make use of the Earth's magnetic field to keep themselves heading further towards deep water. They will wander the open sea for several years, eating and growing at a leisurely pace, before they are ready to breed, and must find their way back to their nesting beaches.

The Earth can be regarded as one giant magnet, with its opposite poles at the North and South Poles, and its magnetic field spanning between them. Therefore any animal with an ability to sense magnetism has a potential means to sense its position on Earth, independently of any visual cues. We already know that many birds sense the Earth's magnetic field through magnetite (a form of iron oxide) crystals carried in the structure of their bills. There are other ways that animals can potentially sense magnetic fields. One possibility is that they possess electroreceptive cells that allow them to sense electromagnetic radiation – this is known in, for example, sharks and rays. Another is through the action of magnetism on a class of proteins called cryptochromes, which are common in nature and undergo chemical changes when exposed to magnetic fields.

As electroreceptors have not been found in sea turtles, their ability to navigate by Earth's magnetic field is probably down to cryptochromes, or magnetite, or both. It has also been suggested that they can direct

themselves by the position and movements of the stars above but no evidence has been found to support this – not that it would be easy to design a suitable and ethical experiment to test it.

One field of research that is very active concerns the actual movements of Leatherbacks, with the Sea Turtle Conservancy's tracking studies of this species dating back to 2003. Their test subjects are adult females tagged when visiting their nesting beaches around Central America. Other studies have followed Leatherbacks that nest in West Africa. The results of the studies show that these animals cover prodigious distances – one animal tracked from Gabon swam 8,000km (4,970 miles) over six months, to the coast of South America, then back again to nest, while other African turtles moved to the southern tip of the African continent and others spent their off-duty time far offshore in the tropical South Atlantic. A turtle from Panama headed east up the coast of North America then out into the Atlantic some 3,000km (1,865 miles) off north Canada, covering more than 12,000km (7,455 miles) in total in just under a year.

Leatherback migrations are proving to be quite complex and varied, with no particular favourite foraging sites. With their great size and power, covering long distances even against strong sea currents is no obstacle to them, so they are free to explore all corners of the world. The main problem they face is marine pollution, in particular plastics. Many adults die after eating large numbers of discarded carrier bags, which look uncannily like jellyfish when hanging in the water column, enough to fool the rather short-sighted turtles. Other hazards they face include entanglement in fishing gear, and the harvesting of their eggs from the nesting beaches.

Map: Studies are revealing that individual Leatherbacks follow different, and complex, migratory routes.

Only female Leatherback Turtles ever return to land, for the important task of egg-laying.

119

Spotted Salamander

Ambystoma maculatum

IUCN Least Concern

Amphibians bridge the gap between land and water in a different way to mammals, birds and reptiles. Many of the animals we have looked at already spend their lives in or over the water but must return to land to breed. For amphibians it is the other way round – most species have to breed in water, and in the early stages of their life are exclusively aquatic, with gills to extract oxygen from the water. Once mature, though, they lose their gills and may abandon their watery cradles and live entirely on the land – until it's time for them to have young of their own, and then they must travel back to the place where it all began.

Relying on warning coloration to put off predators indicates (correctly)
that the Spotted Salamander is not the fastest of animals.

The traveller

Amphibians come in three basic shapes – the tailless, long-limbed frogs and toads, the limbless and wormlike caecilians, and the long-tailed and short-legged newts and salamanders. Members of this last group bear a superficial resemblance to lizards, but have soft moist amphibian skin, and are graceful swimmers but not swift movers on land. The Spotted Salamander, a widespread and common native of woodlands across the eastern USA and Canada, is a quite robust, broad-snouted animal up to 25cm (10in) long. It is strikingly beautiful in its adult form, with shiny black skin marked with two wavering rows of round yellow spots, running either side of its body from head to tail; the spots become more orange at the head end. It is a member of the family Ambystomatidae, or mole salamanders, so called because they live underground, in burrows that they dig into soft earth.

Spotted Salamanders rely on 'vernal' pools for laying their eggs. These are non-permanent pools – they dry out completely in the summertime. This means that the baby salamanders have enough time to reach maturity and leave the pool, but predatory fish cannot colonise it. Fish and amphibians are not happy pond-mates in general, as many fish species have a keen appetite for amphibian eggs and larvae – a point worth remembering when considering whether to add fish to your garden wildlife pond.

Mating in this species is a two-step process. The males arrive first at the pools and begin to produce small, conical packets of sperm, which they encourage the females to take into their cloacas. Fertilisation thus happens internally, and the female then produces a gooey mass of 100–200 eggs, which sticks to underwater plants. This swells up into a sticky ball as its jelly coating absorbs water. Sometimes green algae is visible within the ball – this has a remarkable symbiotic link with the growing embryos, helping to boost their oxygen supply (the jelly layer is excellent at preventing water loss but not so good at letting oxygen in). The algae in return uses carbon dioxide produced by the embryos to drive its photosynthesis.

The larvae hatch after anywhere between 30 and 60 days. They are gilled and limbless, and swim easily with an elegant undulating motion. For a couple of months they stay in the pool, feeding on algae (so no more symbiosis there) and aquatic invertebrates, before the legs grow, the gills are reabsorbed and they leave the fast-shrinking pool. They set up home first within leaf litter near the pool, but as they grow they move further away and begin to dig burrows, which will be their homes for the next few years. They are not ready to breed until three years old, and may live for another 30 years.

The striking coloration of this animal is a warning to predators, and if they do not heed it and try to eat the salamander anyway, they will receive a mouthful of poison, secreted from glands in the skin. The salamander also has the power of autotomy – severed body parts can regrow (up to a point). Most often autotomy involves regrowth of a nipped-off tail but the salamander can also regrow parts of limbs and even some organs. Its mainly subterranean lifestyle does mean that it isn't encountered by most predators very often. It is a predator itself when adult, emerging from its burrows to stalk about the woodland floor and hunt all kinds of small, slow-moving invertebrates, and even the odd very small, very slow vertebrate. Come sunrise, it returns to its burrows, and when winter comes it sleeps underground for the duration – more than six months in the northernmost part of its range.

The journey

So far, so sedentary. But when hibernation is over, the adult salamanders take on a journey that, while short compared to many migrations, is impressive for such a small and stumpy-legged animal. The first rainy night after the ground has thawed is a pretty good bet for being a salamander 'Big Night', with thousands of animals all on the move at once. It might seen counter-intuitive to all migrate at the same time, increasing the chances of drawing predators' attention – but because these animals are moving to their vernal pools to mate, the more of them that join in, the better the chances each one has of getting lucky with the opposite sex. How salamanders and other amphibians navigate is not well-studied, but newts and toads have been shown to orient themselves according to the Earth's magnetic field.

Right: Spotted Salamander egg-mass.

The migration is not epic in terms of distance – few Spotted Salamanders have to travel more than 500m (1,640ft) to reach their pool. Some other species have been recorded going further – 2–3km (1.2–1.9 miles) in the case of some upland salamander species. But if you ever watch one of these animals move you can see that distance is relative. With its long, relatively heavy body and short sprawling legs, it 'walks' very slowly with a greatly exaggerated side-to-side twist that is exhausting just to watch – 90 per cent of its energy seems to go the wrong way. It cannot leap like a frog, and doesn't even have the dogged forward-focused crawl of a toad. At least it does not engage in amplexus – the mating 'clasp' of frogs and toads, whereby a female often has to carry one or more male admirers on her back to the pond.

Spotted Salamanders are at their most vulnerable when on the way to the pool at mating time. They are moving above ground, and they cannot really outrun anything. They have their various self-defence tricks – their warning coloration, poison glands, and the last-ditch measure of autotomy, and no doubt these help keep them safe, but they offer no protection whatsoever against the most deadly of enemies – the car. Where amphibian routes cross roads, the animals may be killed in large numbers, as surveys have shown. The body count on a particular 3.2km (2-mile) stretch of road in Ontario was 32,000 amphibians over just two seasons, while salamander mortality in the breeding season on another road in New York State was 50.3–100 per cent.

These are not trivial losses. Amphibians produce lots of offspring to counteract a high mortality rate in the egg and larval stages, but their populations cannot withstand high adult mortality. Studies indicate that if the annual risk that an adult salamander from a given population will die on the road exceeds just 10 per cent, that could be enough to wipe out the entire population in not very many generations. Conservation bodies urge motorists to take care on spring nights, and to look out for mass movements of salamanders and other amphibians. Where larger roads are involved, bridges or tunnels may be built for the animals to use. In some states there are even road closures on 'Big Nights' to protect the salamanders and ensure that they make it safely to their ponds.

Map shows the distribution of the species. Although its migrations are too short to be shown, they represent tremendous effort nonetheless.

Atlantic Salmon

Salmo salar

IUCN Least Concern

A sleek, colourful salmon battling and leaping its way upstream against a steep white-water torrent, and perhaps narrowly evading the waiting jaws of a Grizzly Bear or talons of a Bald Eagle, is one of the classic images of migration. It's hard to picture a better illustration of the triumph of pure instinct-led determination over all manner of obstacles. This dramatic stage of its migratory journey, though, is just a small part of the adventures experienced by this most impressive of fish during its eventful life. There are many species in the salmon and trout family (Salmonidae, or the 'salmonids'), only a few of which are 'true' salmon, and Atlantic Salmon is the best-known, largest and best-travelled of them.

The urge to spawn drives salmon to astonishing physical efforts.

The traveller

For many of us, this fish is more familiar as a packet of shrink-wrapped pink fillets than as a living animal. It is extensively farmed and could be considered domesticated – farmed salmon begin their lives in freshwater tanks, and are later confined to 'sea cages'. Well-fed and under-exercised, they are plumper than wild salmon, and do not get to experience the migrations of their wild cousins, though they do go through the same switch from fresh to salt-water. Today there is little commercial fishing of wild Atlantic Salmon, after overfishing caused severe declines. Numbers have since begun to recover, and recreational anglers pay big money to access prime salmon rivers and pit their wits against the agile and powerful wild fish.

An adult Atlantic Salmon is a long-bodied, sleek and muscular fish, light silver-grey with a scattering of black spots, and (when ready to spawn) a pink and blue lustre. It has black-edged fins, and large jaws stocked with sharp teeth for seizing its prey – primarily other, smaller fishes and some crustaceans as well. Most adults heading back upstream to spawn are about 70–75cm (28–30in) long and weigh 3.5–5.5kg (7.7–12lb). However, unlike some other salmon species they can live on after their first spawning and continue to grow, so can be much larger than average. There are a handful of records of Atlantic Salmon exceeding 1.5m (5ft) in length and 20kg (44lb) in weight.

The life stages of the Atlantic Salmon begin when adults lay their eggs in spring. The first stage is the alevin, a newly hatched larva that looks more like a tiny, bug-eyed alien than a fish, with a large obvious yolk sac and barely-there fins. It lingers near the hatching site, hiding in gravel on the river bed, and does not feed but gets the nutrition it needs from the remaining contents of its yolk sac. After up to six weeks of this, it has become a fry – its gills are fully developed, its outline is unmistakeably finny and fishy and it is ready to seek food – mainly larval insects at this stage. Salmon fry start to disperse from the breeding site in their quest to eat and eat. They grow rapidly and by the end of their first summer have matured into parr, distinguished by a pattern of vertical stripes. Parr stay in the rivers and streams where they were born, feeding and growing, for one to four years (generally the further north they live, the longer this stage lasts). The next stage is the smolt, characterised by a change in appearance and behaviour – the young salmon lose their stripes and start to head downstream towards the sea, their body chemistry adapting gradually to cope with the increasing salinity of the water. Maturation at sea takes another two or three years, and when each fish has grown large enough to spawn it returns inland at the start of spring.

Atlantic Salmon have spawning sites on both sides of the northern Atlantic, in western Europe and eastern North America. A few populations are landlocked and never migrate to the sea – Atlantic Salmon do not actually 'need' a marine stage to complete their lifecycle. For the rest, when not spawning they range across the whole north Atlantic. They have also been deliberately introduced in western North America, where they pose a risk to native salmonids such as Chinook and Coho Salmon.

The journey

In 1935, the book *Salar the Salmon* by Henry Williamson (celebrated author of *Tarka the Otter*) was published – an enchanting fictionalised account of one salmon's migration to its spawning grounds in Devon. That this book has been a classic of nature writing ever since its publication shows how well-known and much admired the migration of the Atlantic Salmon is.

The young salmon that make it to smolt stage move downstream, encountering increasingly saline water as they near the sea, and move ocean-wards as the tide ebbs. The water itself is no great obstacle to them at this stage as they are very much going with the flow, but they are preyed upon by various aquatic animals including other fish. Eventually, the survivors reach the region of the sea where they will spend the next phase of their lives – for most, this is a region off western Greenland. Marine predators continue to target the smolts but as they increase in size, the risk of predation decreases – they do remain an important food source for Grey Seals though.

The switch to spawning mode occurs when the salmon has reached a large enough size, but the journey does not begin until spring. Now the real miracle happens – from its starting point thousands of kilometres offshore, each salmon finds its way back to land and not only that but to the exact stream where it was born. Investigations into how salmon navigate suggest that they use a range of cues to orient themselves, including magnetoreception (some species have been shown to carry magnetite crystals in their eyes) and, when close to home, a well-developed sense of smell. What exactly they are smelling is a matter of conjecture – perhaps some unique odour from the home stream itself, or perhaps the pheromone signature of its closely related young brothers and sisters that are still living in the stream.

In fact, not every single salmon does return to its natal stream – some have 'near misses' and end up in adjacent streams. A certain margin for error isn't necessarily a bad thing – while some salmon may end up in

streams unsuitable for spawning, others will be luckier, and their navigational errors will allow a population to spread into new areas.

Returning to freshwater requires various bodily changes, and the salmon also has to meet some seriously high energy demands – to fight the current and leap their way over obstacles and up waterfalls all the way home, and to produce eggs or sperm to deploy once it gets there. Only those which really made the most of their time at sea to lay down fat stores and reach prime physical condition will complete the journey in good shape. Their metabolism also changes to use primarily white muscle (suited to short, intense bursts of activity) rather than the more endurance-oriented red muscle. For all their efforts, many will fall victim to predators, including bears, eagles, otters and, of course, *Homo sapiens*.

Those salmon that do survive will (hopefully) spawn in the shallow, gravelly breeding areas, the female placing her eggs in a shallow trench in the gravel, and males then fertilising the eggs. For most salmon species, this is end of story – completely knackered in every sense, they die right after spawning. Atlantic Salmon, though, can survive a spawning event and if they do (though most will not) they return to the sea to build themselves back up, ready to spawn again in a few years' time.

Map: Atlantic Salmon are anadromous, meaning that they are born in freshwater, head far out to sea to mature, and return to their birth stream to spawn.

Even steep waterfalls are not enough to stop a determined salmon on its way home.

European Eel

Anguilla anguilla

IUCN Critically Endangered

Fishermen in Britain and Europe have been catching eels ever since the dawn of fishing, and not necessarily with any great joy. With their tough, twisty and snaky bodies and copious slime, European Eels are not very much fun to handle, and are not really considered among the more delicious fish either (though they have nevertheless long been important as food fishes in parts of Europe, and not just in jellied form). The most intriguing thing about them was that no-one had ever observed a young eel, only full-sized adults. We have now finally begun to piece together the full and extraordinary life history of the European Eel, although whether this knowledge has come in time to save what is now a severely threatened species remains to be seen.

It may be most frequently encountered when skulking in a weedy ditch,
but this is a truly impressive and enigmatic long-distance migrant.

The traveller

The adult European Eel is a typical member of the genus *Anguilla,* the freshwater eels. It has a long, tubular, serpentine body, with small pectoral fins, no pelvic fins, and a long dorsal fin that connects seamlessly with the tail fin. It has very small scales and a generous coating of mucous. Most are about 70cm (28in) long, although occasionally they can grow to 1.5m (5ft). Hunting by night, the European Eel spends the day resting in the thick, muddy substrate of its chosen ditch or pond. It swims slowly with smooth, sinuous wiggles, and when seeking prey it moves close to the bottom, looking for molluscs, crustaceans, small fish and any other aquatic animals that it can catch.

In Europe, this eel may be found in all kinds of freshwater habitats, but especially in lakes, ditches and slow-flowing rivers, where there is a suitably deep layer of soft muddy or sandy substrate in which it can hide. It leads a solitary life of feeding and resting, and slowly grows for about 10–14 years before it is fully mature and ready to spawn – something that it will only do once. Eels that are prevented from migrating to the spawning grounds may live longer, but no natural eel population exists that is cut off from the sea.

Eel life history involves several distinct stages. In its first, larval stage the young eel is known as a 'leptocephalus'. It is a transparent, laterally flattened creature, quite short-bodied and shaped more like a leaf than a snake. With maturity its body changes to the familiar tube shape, but it remains transparent for some time and is known as a 'glass eel'. As it becomes pigmented it is known as an 'elver', and when fully grown and fully pigmented it becomes a 'yellow eel', so called because of its golden tint. It is during this stage that the eel's sexual organs become differentiated – prior to this it has no sex, and whether it becomes male or female is influenced by environmental factors. When fully mature and ready to spawn, it loses this yellow tone and acquires a silvery, counter-shaded coloration (darker above than below, to help disguise its solid shape). Its eyes also become larger and their chemical structure changes. In this final stage it is known as a 'silver eel'.

The journey

It was in 1886 that it was finally ascertained what a leptocephalus really was, when some were kept alive in a tank for some weeks by biologist Yves Delange. Prior to this, the little leaf-shaped fishes, which were found in the north Atlantic, went by the name *Leptocephalus brevirostris*, but Delange discovered that they were in fact the juvenile form of *Anguilla anguilla* when they matured into glass eels. This was the first piece in the jigsaw puzzle of the eel life-cycle.

Knowing that larval eels were found in the north Atlantic, the Danish biologist Johannes Schmidt carried out a number of expeditions in that region in the early 20th century. He was able to narrow down the search for the European Eel's spawning grounds by sampling leptocephali from different parts of the Atlantic, finding the smallest larvae in the region of the Sargasso Sea. This area is believed to be the main or only spawning ground – the destination for migrating silver eels.

The journey they undertake is longer than 6,000km (3,730 miles), and they are fully physically committed to it, having undergone various physical changes to help them survive travel in the open sea. The change from golden to silver helps to camouflage them, and the changes to their eye structure are adaptations to the kind of light conditions they will encounter at sea – larger eyes with altered retinal pigments, to cope with dimmer and bluer light. More profoundly, their gut actually disappears, rendering them unable to feed, so they need to have sufficient energy stores before setting off, but they save energy on the various metabolic processes associated with feeding. They are estimated to cover about 15km (9 miles) a day in their journey to the spawning grounds.

They presumably die fairly soon after spawning – it is not known for certain exactly what happens, but with no way to feed their fate is sealed. They leave behind a new generation of leptocephali, which drift and feed in the open sea until they have become glass eels. Now, migration inland begins. Glass eels are still adapted for life in marine waters, but as they gather around estuaries and other coastal areas and prepare to head inland, they start to change, acquiring pigmentation and becoming elvers.

Elvers travelling inland are amazingly adept at overcoming obstacles – in their way they are as impressive as Atlantic Salmon. They can travel over land as well as through water, as long as the crossing is reasonably

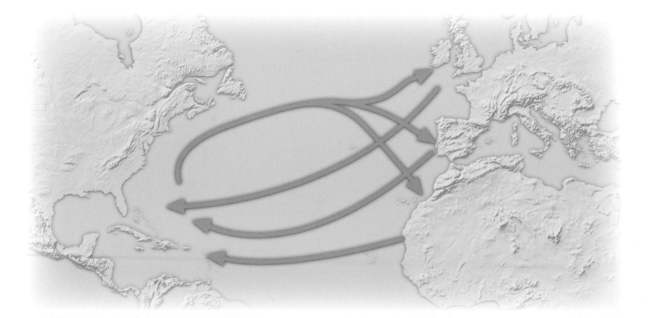

Right: Young eels, or elvers, make a slippery meal for many predators – in this case a Common Kingfisher. The overfishing of elvers by humans is one possible cause of this species' recent catastrophic decline.

short and the ground reasonably wet – rain-soaked fields of long grass are easily crossed. They pile up at bottlenecks and climb over each other to get over boulders and other objects blocking their path. They are, of course, highly vulnerable to predators at this time, but perhaps no more than they are in earlier life stages. Once settled in the lake, river or pond of their choice they stand a good chance of making it to maturity.

Given that the European Eel seemed a ubiquitous fish of all slow and still waters across Europe just a few decades ago, it is shocking that it is now classed as Critically Endangered – in serious risk of extinction in the near future. A very severe decline has been observed, primarily through reduced harvests of the immature glass eels that are caught and then matured in captivity for the food trade. It is not clear why the decline is happening but pollution, overfishing, parasitic infection (in particular by the nematode worm *Anguillicola crassus*, brought to Europe with imported Japanese Eels), climate change affecting larval survival, and blocking of migratory routes are all probably involved. The latter problem has been addressed in some nations by the provision of 'eel ladders' to help the animals negotiate blockages. The other problems will require a co-ordinated international effort – fishing quotas are now imposed and trade in the eel is now banned outside Europe, and there are very early signs that these measures are having a positive impact.

Map: In a reversal of the Atlantic Salmon's lifecycle, European Eels are catadromous, being born far out in the Atlantic Ocean, then heading inland up rivers to mature, before returning to the sea to spawn.

Monarch

Danaus plexippus

IUCN Not assessed

In the USA, most of the states have their own nominated 'state insect', as well as the better-known 'state bird', and seven states have selected the Monarch butterfly. This glorious tiger-striped creature is a common species in North America, but it also has the distinction of being a regular, albeit very rare, visitor to Britain on the opposite side of the Atlantic. Only a handful of insect species have ever made this prodigious journey, and the Monarch is notable for managing it pretty much every year, often arriving alongside small birds from North America that have been pushed across by strong winds. Although this is vagrancy rather than migration, Monarchs across most of their range are also true migrants and are famous for their long-distance journey, the full distance undertaken by successive generations of butterflies with the baton handed to new recruits along the way.

Monarchs cluster together on their roosting trees.
Their warning coloration helps keep predators away.

The traveller

A spectacular very large butterfly with orange, black-striped wings and a black, white-spotted body, the Monarch is well-named. This insect is extremely striking in both larval and adult forms, and the adult butterfly would be quite unmistakeable if a number of Monarch-mimics had not evolved alongside it. Its bright colours and pattern are aposematic – a warning to predators that it is not to be eaten. As a caterpillar it feeds on milkweed plants, which contain toxins called cardiac glycosides. This doesn't harm the caterpillar itself, but large quantities of the toxins build up in its body and produce unpleasant consequences for any predator that eats it – they also make the caterpillar taste so bad that few predators would even reach the point of ingesting it. The adult butterfly carries the same evil-tasting payload, with toxins stored in its wings as well as its body so that it stands a good chance of surviving an attack by a predator that has not yet learned to avoid Monarchs.

The Viceroy butterfly is very similar to the Monarch, and the two are Müllerian mimics of each other – that is to say that both are poisonous and bad-tasting and benefit from their similarity to each other. A predator that has had a bad experience with a Monarch is likely to also avoid Viceroys, and vice versa. Monarch caterpillars are quite different to Viceroy caterpillars, although both are boldly marked. Monarch caterpillars sport bold black, white and yellow stripes from their second instar onwards, but the egg and first-instar caterpillar are translucent green, lacking aposematic coloration, as they have not acquired the protective toxins.

Adult Monarchs, like other butterflies in the family Nymphalidae, seem at first glance to defy the 'insects have six legs' rule, as they appear to have only four. The front pair are present but are tiny and held against the sides of the head. The sexes are subtly different, males having narrower stripes and also a dark patch of androconial (pheromone-producing) scales on their hindwings – a so-called 'scent brand'.

Monarchs are found from southern Canada down to northern South America – south of there they are replaced by the similar Southern Monarch. They have also spread to islands in the south Pacific and to Australia, and eastwards to Iberia and north Africa. On Oahu, Hawaii, where Monarchs were first found in the 19th century, a stunning white morph makes up a significant proportion of the population. It is not known whether the spread of the Monarch has been entirely natural, or down to being introduced (deliberately or accidentally) by people. Their regular arrivals in Britain do show that the insects have the power to make significant sea crossings under their own steam (with a bit of help from the wind).

Overleaf: These lovely butterflies are stunning enough when seen individually, but en masse they create a breathtaking spectacle.

The journey

Like most insects, Monarchs are not blessed with a long life. They do not even have the extended childhood (caterpillar-hood?) of some butterfly species – the entire life-cycle from egg to adult can be completed in as little as four weeks. The adults themselves would be lucky to live four more weeks, and as this is the only truly mobile life-stage, the potential for travel is limited, compared to larger animals. Nevertheless, the entire eastern Monarch population of North America does travel, the most northerly of them moving more than 7,000km (4,350miles) to wintering grounds in Mexico. Western populations also migrate – over shorter distances but still several thousand kilometres. Completing this journey is one of the most astounding achievements of any animal on Earth.

When summer nears its end, the new generation of adult Monarchs undergoes a physiological change, triggered by cues such as shortening daylight hours, reduced temperatures, and the dying back of the milkweed plants on which they lay their eggs. Their bodies become optimised for travel, with reproductive behaviours and physiological processes repressed, and their bodies store up as much fuel in the form of fat as possible. They also become more social, tending to feed together by day and roost together at night. Autumn migrants are funnelled down particular routes where conditions (weather, availability of flowers on which to feed, and suitable prevailing winds) are best. Once they arrive at the wintering grounds, they roost for several weeks in huge gatherings, clustering together in the same favourite trees, so densely sometimes that the tree appears to have butterflies for foliage. Not surprisingly, this extraordinary sight is a major tourist attraction. Most eastern Monarchs roost in an area of Mexico that is now protected as the Monarch Butterfly Biosphere Reserve, part of which is open to the public – visitors are closely supervised though, as the butterflies are very vulnerable to disturbance. Western populations winter mainly in California.

By February, the signs of spring are triggering changes in the Monarchs, and their bodies change again,

preparing to breed. They begin to move north, mating and egg-laying on the way, and as each generation dies, a new one takes its place on the migration. The butterflies that finally arrive back in the summer areas are four or five generations removed from those that travelled south the year before, so prior experience can be absolutely ruled out as a means of navigating. Studies show that they seem to find their way by using a combination of the sun's position, and sensitivity to the Earth's magnetic field, through magnetism-sensitive structures in their antennae.

Although not assessed by the IUCN, the Monarch is causing some concern among conservationists. As with other migrants, it has different needs on its summering and wintering grounds and on its migration route as well. The milkweeds on which it lays its eggs are in decline, thanks to agricultural changes. Unsuitable weather conditions, including drought, can devastate populations at all stages of their annual journey, and climate change increases the likelihood of this happening. Most wintering areas do at least enjoy strict protection.

Map: Monarchs from across North America funnel south into Mexico for the winter.

Above: Monarch caterpillar on its foodplant, milkweed.

Hummingbird Hawkmoth

Macroglossum stellatarum

IUCN Not assessed

As we have seen, some species of hummingbirds are long-distance migrants – an impressive feat for such tiny birds. However, none has yet been known to cross over from their native Americas to Europe or Africa, so any reports of hummingbirds seen in these areas must be treated with scepticism, no matter how convinced the observer may be. The most likely suspect for such mistaken identity is not a bird at all but a moth – the beautiful little Hummingbird Hawkmoth, which looks and behaves uncannily like a real hummingbird, and is also an impressive migrant in its own right.

Its ability to hover motionless while feeding makes this moth
a favourite subject among wildlife photographers.

The traveller

Southern Europe in summer is a great place to watch Hummingbird Hawkmoths in action. Pick a sunny day, find a stand of suitable nectar-rich flowering plants, such as lavenders, and wait. With luck, a moth will arrive soon, and treat you to an exhibition of precision flying as it hovers around the flowers, probing individual blossoms with its tongue while its fast-vibrating wings flash vivid orange and produce an audible hum. Its buzzing hover, upright stance, apparent lack of legs (as they are neatly tucked in), flared and flattened 'tail' (actually the tip of its abdomen), obvious dark-centred eyes and long, curving black bill-like tongue, all create a convincing impression of the bird from which it takes its name – only its antennae really look a bit at odds. If you see one at rest though, standing on its six legs with its brown forewings concealing the more colourful hindwings and lying flat over its back in the normal moth manner, you would wonder if it is even the same creature.

Although a biggish moth, the Hummingbird Hawkmoth is one of the smaller hawkmoths – the group includes some of the largest, heaviest and fastest-flying moths in the world. The 'hummer' is also one of relatively few hawkmoths that is active in the daytime rather than at night, so while some other hawkmoths have a similar feeding style, they are unlikely to be observed by most of us. Hummingbird Hawkmoths, though, relish heat and sunshine, and though they also feed at dusk, they stay active in midday temperatures hot enough to send most insects into the shade to rest or even into a state of prolonged inactivity. The heat generated in their flight muscles can exceed 40°C (104°F), which is probably close to the absolute operational limit for an insect.

This moth lays its eggs on bedstraws and related plants. Each female produces up to 200 eggs, each placed on a separate plant (so egg-laying takes up a great deal of her time). They are camouflaged to resemble the host plant's flower buds and hatch after about a week, producing a yellow caterpillar which as it grows and moults becomes green, with a yellow side-stripe and a thorn-like spike at the rear (a typical hawkmoth trait). It can mature in as little as three weeks if the weather is warm enough for it to feed uninterrupted. It climbs to the ground to pupate among leaf litter. The pupa is glossy brown with a long thin loop running from the head-end to the middle of its back – this is destined to be its tongue. The pupal stage lasts a couple of weeks. Adults live a few weeks, although those that emerge at the end of summer may live through the winter in cooler areas, as they hibernate.

The adult moth has grey-brown forewings but orange hind-wings. The wings are quite narrow and look smallish for the size of the insect. The tip of its abdomen is black with white spots, and has long hairs that stick out downwards and sideways, making it look longer and wider than it is – this shape is likely to help with flight control. The tongue (or more accurately proboscis) is black and shiny, and when extended is straight with a bend part-way along to angle it into a flower. When the moth withdraws, the proboscis retracts in a neat coil.

The foraging tactic of this moth is reported to be 'trap-lining' – another trait it has in common with hummingbirds. It works a regular circuit, moving the same way along a line of flowering plants and only visiting each blossom once – and the following day it repeats the circuit. This gives the flowers time to replenish their nectar stores, ready for their pollinator to return. The moths are also capable of learning new associations. Experiments wherein they were offered variable amounts of sugar-water from differently coloured artificial 'flowers' showed that they prefer blue or violet blooms but are quick to switch preferences if a different colour is associated with a better reward.

Hummingbird Hawkmoths may be found right across Europe, most of Asia except the extreme north and south, and a fair chunk of north Africa. However, they only reach the northern band of this range in summer (they cannot survive cold winters), and in variable numbers, while they are only in the far south in winter. In the central band of their range, they are present year-round and in warmer areas may be on the wing all year as well.

The journey

Hummingbird Hawkmoths spread northwards during the course of the summer, to make the most of good feeding areas outside their year-round range. In winter they do the same thing but moving southwards. Many individuals do not move any distance at all, as they find all they need in the area where they are born, but if numbers are very high, this can trigger an emigration as individuals seek out untapped resources.

Map: There is much variation from year to year in the numbers of Hummingbird Hawkmoths heading north, and in the distances they travel.

Hummingbird Hawkmoths cannot survive the winter in cooler climates, including the British Isles. Numbers arriving in Britain are very variable year on year, but in good years many thousands make landfall along the south and east coasts of England, often in the company of other migratory Lepidoptera, such as Clouded Yellow and Painted Lady butterflies.

The distance covered by any individual Hummingbird Hawkmoth is highly variable, but the species has occurred in Newfoundland – a distance of more than 3,000km (1,865 miles) from the nearest point in Europe – which shows that it is capable of surviving and carrying enough fuel for seriously long flights. However, there seems to be no regular pattern to their movements beyond a general tendency to spread north in summer and south in winter. It is likely that this species is irruptive, in a similar way to the Bohemian Waxwing, and moves off to new areas when food is in short supply (either because of a lack of flowers, or a higher-than-usual moth population). How they identify north and south, though, is not known for certain, but some other lepidopteran species have been shown to navigate through magnetoreception, and through checking the position of the sun.

Above: The moths forage along a set route, allowing enough time for each flower to refill its nectar stores.

Madagascan Sunset Moth

Chrysiridia rhipheus

IUCN Not assessed

Everyone knows that among Lepidoptera, the butterflies are the colourful glamour-pusses and the moths are their dingy, nocturnal cousins. Except that one of the moths clearly has aspirations to be counted among the butterflies. Many moths of the family Uraniidae are large, day-flying, and boast extravagantly ornamented and outrageously coloured wings – unsurprisingly they were originally thought to be swallowtail butterflies when first discovered. The Madagascan Sunset Moth, found only on Madagascar, is arguably the most stunning of them all, and many lepidopterists rate it as more beautiful than any butterfly. It is also a notable migrant, crossing its island home twice a year in rhythm with the growth seasons of its food-plants.

The traveller

Nature has not come up with many more glorious creatures than the Madagascan Sunset Moth. This lovely insect has large technicoloured wings, with iridescent tiger-stripe bands of blue, green, yellow and red on a black background. All these colours, though, are not 'real'. They are created not through coloured pigment but through light refraction from special curved scales on the wings. Variation in the scales' microstructure creates the dazzling array of colours, and it is possible that the moth can perceive light polarisation and thus position itself and its wings in the optimal position to show itself off. The hind-wings bear three long and three short projections or 'tails'. Their function is possibly to create the impression of antennae, leading predators to mistake the outer edge of the hind-wing for a head, and direct attacks there rather than at the actual head, giving the insect a chance to escape.

Being colourful and day-flying does suggest, though, that the Madagascan Sunset Moth has little fear of predators, and indeed its colours are aposematic – warning that it is very poisonous and best avoided. The toxins in its body are obtained from the plants it eats when it is a caterpillar. It feeds on *Omphalea* plants, most importantly *O. oppositifilia*. This plant and its relatives are members of the spurge or euphorbia family, which are so poisonous (leaves, fruits, the lot) that almost no other animals can cope with them. Four *Omphalea* species occur on Madagascar and the sunset moth caterpillars will feed on all of them, eating all parts of the plant. The caterpillars constantly produce sticky silk from their mouthparts as they move around the plant – this helps keep them from slipping off the smooth leaves, and gives them a means to climb back up if they do. When ready to pupate, the caterpillars drop down to the ground and spin a light silk cocoon, within which they pupate. The moth breeds all year round and can complete its life-cycle in as little as three months.

There is a constant struggle underway between the caterpillar and its host-plants – the one needing to eat, the other needing to not be eaten. *Omphalea oppositifilia* plants that have gone unmolested for some generations have considerably lower toxicity than those that have been targeted more recently, which suggests that the caterpillars survive on a knife-edge. Moth populations crash periodically, and this is probably due to extreme elevated toxicity in some populations of the food-plant, killing off caterpillars and forcing adult moths to search more widely for less lethal nurseries in which to place their eggs. It is also possible that plants under sustained attack by caterpillars can release chemicals that attract parasitic wasps, which lay their eggs on the caterpillars with deadly results.

The journey

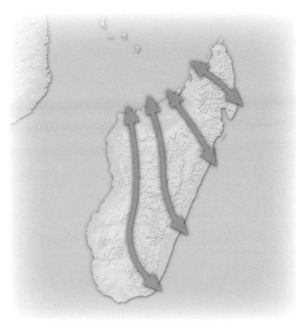

Moving around to find untouched populations of *Omphalea* is the moths' first line of defence against a host-plant that has the ability to fight back. But the moth would have to migrate anyway, or spend part of the year inactive, as the different *Omphalea* species have different growth seasons.

The four species of *Omphalea* have different distributions in Madagascar. *O. palmata* and *O. occidentalis* occur in the west and north-west, *O. ankaranensis* only in the far north, and the key host-plant species, *O. oppositifilia*, is found only on the east side of the island. During their growth season, *O. palmata* and *O. occidentalis* are the main host plants for the Madagascan Sunset Moth. When these two are no longer available, the moths migrate to the west side of the island to exploit *O. oppositifilia*. This species, unlike the other three, is evergreen. The moths could therefore lay their eggs on it all year round, but they do better if they switch their attentions to the other *Omphalea* species when these become available. This reduces the chances of *O. oppositifilia* populations retaliating by upping their toxicity – instead, they are given some respite and in response the toxin levels in their leaves subsides. Manufacturing high volumes of toxins seems to be quite a significant demand for the plants to meet, and only worth doing when their foliage is being eaten by lots of hungry caterpillars. Lowered toxins then makes life easier for the moths when they return from their holiday on the west side of the island.

On migration, the moths are gregarious and form roosting flocks by night, resting in a butterfly-like stance with the wings pressed together above the back. When on the move they travel above the canopy, perhaps making use of the wind to save energy. They descend when they need to feed and visit predominantly white-petalled flowers, though curiously they avoid the flowers of *Omphalea*. Not all the moths make the 500–600km (310–370-mile) trip across Madagascar, but larger-scale movements occur when the moth population is higher than average.

The relationship between the Madagascan Sunset Moth and the *Omphalea* plants is an interesting example of migration as a tactic in an evolutionary arms-race. When one species depends very closely on just one other, they are locked in a fast-moving struggle to out-manoeuvre each other, the penalty for failure being risk of extinction. By migrating when necessary to make use of secondary host-plants, the moth takes the pressure off itself and its main host-plant.

Overleaf: Madagascar has been much harmed by over-intensive agriculture but still has some extensive wild places.

Map: These moths cross from east to west to make use of different food-plants at different times of year.

Desert Locust

Schistocerca gregaria

IUCN Least Concern

According to the Bible, the Israelites were saved from starvation – not once but twice – when a migrating flock of quails pitched down in their camp. Whether you see this as a divine miracle or not is up to you, but it is certainly not outside the bounds of possibility. Quails are migratory, and migrating birds of any kind may make unscheduled stop-offs en route, especially when the weather closes in. When it involves a very large number of birds, such an event is known in birding circles as a 'fall'. But a sudden arrival of masses of hungry insects goes by a more doom-laden name, and the devastating plagues of locusts described in the Bible are very much founded in reality.

The traveller

The insect order Orthoptera contains the grasshoppers, crickets and locusts, and a few other similar hopping or digging creatures. These are striking and often large insects, built for movement with their long powerful hind-legs for prodigious leaping and, in adults of most species, well-developed wings that can carry them considerable distances. They have large eyes and prominent antennae, and some hear very well and also make sounds for communication with others of their kind, by rubbing various body parts together (this is known as stridulation). All this well-developed sensory equipment points to an animal with quite complex behaviours. Most of the species are strictly vegetarian and have long, big heads accommodating their strong mouthparts, used to crunch through tough vegetation.

Orthopterans' development is a three-stage process, or incomplete metamorphosis – there is no pupa stage. Instead the larva (which has well-developed legs and looks much like a wingless adult) goes through a series of moults to accommodate its growing body. It leaves behind its old skin, or exuvia – a perfect paper-thin shell – and when freshly emerged it is temporarily soft-bodied, allowing for some expansion. The final moult sees the emergence of the full-sized and winged adult, which after a further short period of maturation is ready to breed. The Desert Locust is up to 6cm (2.4in) long when adult, with long wings marked with dark bands and speckles. It is mostly yellow, with some black patches, when fully mature, although nymphs are camouflaged to match the vegetation on which they feed.

The Desert Locust is found over a wide area of Africa, the Middle East and west Asia. The core of its range is a band stretching from Mauritania across Arabia to north-west India, but it can spread much more widely at times. This insect is a Jekyll and Hyde character. When its population density is low, it leads a fairly inoffensive, sedentary and solitary life. However, when numbers build up in a certain area, proximity to other locusts sets off a series of physical and behavioural changes. It switches to its gregarious phase and this leads to the formation of swarms.

The journey

The term 'locust' is used to describe a variety of orthopterans that are not necessarily closely related but exhibit strongly gregarious and migratory behaviour. Several of these are potentially problematic as crop pests, but none more so than the Desert Locust. Major swarms can devastate vast areas, and cause famines. Controlling these outbreaks once they get going can be very difficult, so it is important to build as complete an understanding as possible of the locust's biology and ecology.

Above: Mature locusts have long, strong
wings enabling them to fly long distances.

Overleaf: A farmer's nightmare
– a locust swarm in full flow.

Migrating locust swarms have their genesis among the flightless larvae, or 'hoppers'. These normally have no particular attraction to each other, but when numbers build up and competition for the dwindling resources increases, they encounter each other more and more. The increased close contact stimulates them to release a pheromone that sparks a tendency to group together rather than stay apart. When this happens, the hoppers change appearance as well as behaviour, going from a camouflaged green or brown colour to a more adult-like black-and-yellow pattern. It is thus easy to spot hoppers in their 'gregarious' phase. When the gregarious hoppers mature and have grown fully developed wings, they take to the air in swarms, in search of new places to feed.

A swarm on the move travels with the wind. It can move quickly, covering up to 200km (125 miles) a day, and can also move at heights of up to 2,000m (6,560ft) above sea level before the air is too cold for the insects to survive. This is high enough to get over many obstacles, though not the great mountain ranges. The swarms are incredibly dense, covering up to holding up to 1,200 sq km (463 sq miles) with up to 80 million individual locusts per square kilometre. With all their billions of hungry mouths, these swarms will make short work of a growing crop, and almost anything will do. Each locust needs to eat about 2g of vegetation a day (its own weight) and it can live for up to six months.

The last major plague of Desert Locusts occurred in summer 2004, following heavy rain across north-western Africa in 2003, which produced a strong flush of vegetation in desert areas and allowed the locusts to breed very successfully. The swarms began to appear in early 2004, and by summer had spread as far afield as the Canary Islands, Portugal and Crete. Efforts to control them across 20 countries cost an estimated US$400 million. A cold and dry winter helped to interrupt the locusts' breeding cycle and prevented total catastrophe, but some countries in the Sahel region still lost up to half of their harvest to the insects. This precipitated a food crisis affecting millions of people.

Powerful insecticides are the method of choice to deal with swarms. These have their drawbacks, being a rather 'scorched-earth' approach that destroys numerous other animals (including some that would prey on the locusts), but in the grip of a plague such desperate measures are vital to save communities from famine. Monitoring locusts in quiet periods is necessary to see the early signs of swarm formation. A promising means of biological control to be used at this early stage has been in development for some decades. This is an Orthoptera-specific infectious fungus, *Metarhizium acridum*. It can be administered to the gregarious hoppers in spray form. The diseased insects die within days, and before that they are easy prey for birds in their weakened state (the fungal infection does not affect birds or other predators). It has also been found that the pheromone that keeps adult swarms together differs from that which encourages the hoppers to band together – and when hoppers are exposed to the adult version they seem to lose the ability to detect their own pheromones, resulting in cessation of the gregarious behaviour. This could potentially be used in the fight to stop swarms before they start.

The ecology of 'irruptive' animals like Desert Locusts shows how successful migration and dispersal can be as a strategy to cope with food shortages and the need to spread to new habitats. But because locusts are such a serious threat to our own ecology, we must do all we can to stop these particular migrations in their tracks. Locust plagues show us that we do not dominate nature as much as we may like to think.

Map: In plague years, locusts spread out from their core range to reach nearly the whole of northern and central Africa, Arabia and beyond.

Above: Individually, an innocuous insect. Collectively, one of the most damaging species on the planet, at least as far as humans are concerned.

Globe Skimmer

Pantala flavescens

IUCN Least Concern

Many insects are expert fliers, but none impress quite as much as the dragonflies. These fearsome and (for invertebrates) clever little predators combine startling straight-line speed with the great manoeuvrability necessary to chase down their prey (all other flying insects). Watch a dragonfly on the wing doing its stuff and you'll see it streaking along in fast powered flight, performing long graceful glides, hovering on the spot, moving vertically and even backwards, and executing pin-precise turns on a sixpence. Anyone who has ever stood around waiting for a hawker dragonfly to stop patrolling its territory and settle for a photograph will know that dragonflies also have incredible endurance. For such accomplished aeronauts, long-distance migration is a doddle, and one species in particular is arguably the most accomplished traveller of all, large or small, on the face of the Earth.

A member of the darter/chaser dragonfly group, the Globe Skimmer packs a lot of punch for its relatively small size.

The traveller

Dragonflies and the smaller damselflies make up the order Odonata. This name – 'toothed jaws' – is a clue to their fiercely predatory ways. Even when they are tiny larvae, dragonflies are mobile and active hunters. Adult dragonflies and damselflies lay their eggs in water, and the larvae may spend years slowly growing and feeding, with some species becoming large enough to prey on tadpoles and small fish. Once they reach full size, they are ready to climb out of the water and out of their larval skins, and begin their much shorter but airborne adult lives.

Several species of dragonflies are noted migrants. In Britain we have the Migrant Hawker, which used to occur just as a rare visitor but over the last few decades has spread and colonised in earnest. Hot on its heels is the Southern Migrant Hawker, not yet established here but arriving in summer with increasing regularity at sites in the south and east. Another aptly named visitor is the Vagrant Emperor, which comes up to us from Africa in years when it has a population boom.

The best-named of all the migrant dragonflies, though, is the Globe Skimmer. This species is a relatively small dragonfly, with a big head and slim body (brownish in males, yellowish in females), and unusually long broad wings for its size – its genus name, *Pantala,* means 'all wings'. It belongs to the family Libellulidae, home of the darters, skimmers and chasers. These dragonflies are (usually) less hyperactive than the hawkers and enjoy a good long rest in the sun, but several of the group are notable migrants. The Globe Skimmer has the most extensive world range of them all, and indeed of any Odonata. It can be found regularly across virtually the entire Southern Hemisphere and a reasonable wedge of the northern – anywhere where the mean annual temperature is 20°C (68°F). Additionally, it has occurred as a vagrant in many countries beyond its core range.

Unlike some of the larger and less widespread dragonflies, its life-cycle is rather condensed – the larvae can mature in as little as six weeks. This means that it can make use of small, temporary pools. Eggs are laid in clutches of 1,000 or more, in all kinds of water bodies – females have even been observed egg-laying in swimming pools. Assuming the site selected is a bit more natural than that, the underwater phase of life is characterised by non-stop, unfussy feeding on whatever small aquatic creatures it can catch. When it matures, it climbs out of the water up some emergent vegetation or other suitable surface, its skin splits, and the adult insect inside carefully backflips its way out. Once its wings and body have become pumped full of fluid and become firm, it is ready to take its maiden flight, and a few days later it is sexually mature and ready to seek a mate.

Overleaf: Globe Skimmers originating from India may not make landfall until they reach the coast of Madagascar (pictured).

The journey

Globe Skimmers are well known to be serious wanderers. Records of them in northern Europe are regarded with some skepticism as they could have arrived with cargo (there is evidence that the Sahara and its associated prevailing winds may be a significant barrier for them). However, their presence on very remote islands, such as Easter Island, suggest a very pioneering spirit. The Globe Skimmer was the first dragonfly to be found on Bikini Atoll after the fauna there was devastated by nuclear tests in the 1940s and 1950s. It has been recorded flying at a staggering altitude of 6,200m (20,340ft) in the Himalayas, higher than any other dragonfly. In autumn, large swarms may be seen on the move, making use of thermals (rising air currents) to gain height, allowing them to glide down a long distance without significant energy costs. But it is only very recently that the true extent of this dragonfly's global movements has been investigated.

There are many species of animals in the world that are very widely distributed. The Osprey, for example, as we saw earlier, is an exceptionally widespread migratory bird. It breeds over much of the Northern Hemisphere and winters over much of the Southern Hemisphere. Tracking studies show in detail what we already knew in outline from ringing studies – that birds nesting in North America migrate to South America, and those nesting in Europe migrate to West Africa. These two separate populations have been shown to have consistent genetic differences, because they do not intermingle, and they are classed as distinct subspecies.

It would be very reasonable to assume that a look at the genetics of the Globe Skimmer would produce similar distinctions between the populations on different continents. Perhaps the differences would be even more obvious, because of the dragonfly's shorter generation time. However, a study published in 2016 made the startling announcement that this is not the case. The researchers sampled Globe Skimmers from specimens taken from Texas, eastern Canada, Japan, Korea, India and South America, and found that they

were genetically indistinguishable. Across its entire vast world range, the genetic profile of the Globe Skimmer lacks significant variation. This can only be explained by the dragonflies' gene pools mingling freely, which in turn means that this tiny creature must undertake tremendous overseas crossings of thousands of kilometres – not just occasionally, but regularly.

Why would the Globe Skimmer put itself through this? There's no doubt that having a vast, widespread and freely interbreeding population is a good way for a species to 'future-proof' itself against localised disasters. But animals don't act for the benefit of their species – their motivation is to pass on their genes. The fact that this species can use transient pools does give it great freedom to travel – it is not tied to any particular habitat and can move with the weather and be reasonably sure that it will find somewhere to lay its eggs. The same behaviour is seen in other migratory and irruptive dragonflies. But the leap to regular continent-hopping is less easily explained. The recent genetic study has sparked great scientific interest in this unassuming but world-beating insect, and no doubt we shall soon uncover more of its secrets.

Map: This species has no particular migratory route but wanders extensively across the southern half of the planet.

Below: Studies have revealed that Globe Skimmers around the world are genetically indistinguishable, showing they mix and interbreed freely.

Caribbean Spiny Lobster

Panulirus argus

IUCN Data Deficient

So far in this book we have looked at animals that make their migrations by swimming through the sea, walking across the land, and flying through the air. The Caribbean Spiny Lobster represents a fourth, much smaller category – animals that migrate by walking underwater. This rather ungainly marine creature's migrations are well-observed phenomena, but their purpose and triggers are still largely a mystery.

It is still not clear why these lobsters make their regular walking migrations.

The traveller

Lobsters are decapod crustaceans, a group that also includes the crabs, crayfish, prawns and shrimps. These are active underwater animals with tough exoskeletons, strong walking legs, and prominent antennae. Their usual mode of life is scavenger or predator. In many respects they are the underwater equivalent of the insects, with the important difference (for us and them) that we find them much more delicious than insects.

We think of lobsters as large long-bodied creatures, with one of their five pairs of legs modified into a pair of pincers, to seize and cut edible items. However, a number of groups of decapods bear the name 'lobster', without necessarily being closely related. The spiny or rock lobsters (family Palinuridae) resemble the true clawed lobsters at first glance, having the long segmented body ending with a flattened paddle-like 'tail' fan around the tip of the body (the telson), but they do not have claws. They do have very long fine antennules and even longer, stout antennae, the bases of which are covered with the spines that give the group its name. Spiny lobsters live in seas with reefs, mangroves or other complex underwater 'architecture' that offers lots of hiding places. They occur in warm seas all around the world, with the Caribbean Spiny Lobster found in the western Atlantic.

After hatching from its egg, a young spiny lobster starts life as a tiny speck within the constellation of tiny specks that is zooplankton, drifting freely in the water. Viewed under a microscope, this larva or phyllosoma is a stunning little creature with a mass of very long hair-like legs, its body translucent to reveal all its delicate complexity. No other decapods go through a similar larval stage – they all have the shape of their adult selves from birth. Phyllosomae moult several times before transforming into a miniature adult-like form, the puerulus, and beginning to pursue an adult like life, on the sea-bed. They start out living among algal beds or other vegetation before moving to the reefs where they find suitable crevices in which to live, usually at depths no deeper than 90m (295ft).

The Caribbean Spiny Lobster is nocturnal and solitary. It needs to be, as it is prey for many marine animals. Lacking claws, its main line of defence is to rush into a sheltering crevice, but it can also make a screeching, rasping sound by rubbing part of an antenna against its exoskeleton, which may alarm a predator long enough for the lobster to escape. It is also hunted for food by humans. In some areas divers go after it for fun, killing it with spears or catching it by hand after luring it out of its hiding place by tickling it with a stick. However, most are caught by more conventional means – in lobster pots, baited with smelly meat. In parts of its range it is of great economic importance. For example, in Cuba it accounts for 60 per cent of all gross fisheries income.

The journey

Spiny lobsters don't stay put in their favourite part of the reef forever. They have been observed to make mass migrations across the sea-bed, which are quite something to behold. The animals march along in single-file conga lines of about 50 animals, each keeping in contact with the lobster in front using its long antennules. They move with remarkable purposefulness and synchronicity, like a single bizarre multi-legged creature snaking its way along the sea-bed. The line progresses at quite a rate considering these are small animals working against water resistance, covering about 1km (0.6 miles) an hour, each lobster moving with almost a galloping gait. If threatened, the line stays together but forms a protective curve to keep the predator away.

While the migrations have been observed by scuba divers for many years, what we are only just beginning to learn is how and why they begin, and where they end. There have been some tagging studies on adult Caribbean and other spiny lobsters (which have similar migratory behaviours). Fishermen are encouraged to send in details whenever they catch a tagged lobster. Most of those that are found again are recovered very close to where they were tagged, but some have trotted as far as 300km (185 miles) (straight-line distance) across the sea-bed. The general tendency seems to be for female lobsters at least to move to deeper water in winter, probably because deep water stays warmer and this helps the eggs they are carrying to develop more quickly.

More recently, tagged juveniles (from one to four years old) have been shown to make similar journeys. Foraging in shallower water probably gives richer pickings than deeper water, as there tends to be more animal life in general in the warmer shallows. However, the lobsters' activity is reduced when water temperature drops, so moving to the warmer depths for winter is a way around this, even though there is less for them to eat. Worsening autumn weather can also make foraging in shallower water more difficult, as storms can stir up sandbanks and the water is generally more turbulent.

Spiny lobsters have been shown to be able to sense magnetic fields, and this presumably helps guide their migration. They are also able to sense shifts in temperature and water pressure, and their keen sense of smell picks up changes in the water's chemical balance. What they cannot do is see where they are going – except for the leader of the line. This individual has the most difficult job – leading the way, pushing through the greatest water resistance and lacking the protection of another lobster's body at its front end. Those behind are more sheltered, and perhaps they also help push the leader along. Overall, moving in lines means energy efficiency, and the individuals with the most powerful drive to migrate naturally find themselves leading the dance.

Caribbean Spiny Lobster migration is a famous phenomenon, which you may see for yourself if you go scuba-diving around Florida or the Caribbean at the right time of year. This may be a better way to acquaint yourself with the species than by eating it, as there are signs from the size of fishery takes in some countries that it is generally declining, and over-exploitation may be a cause (along with climate change, and disease outbreaks). Protection during the spawning season in spring, and rules on the minimum size of animals that can be taken, are among the measures being implemented to help protect it.

Map: Caribbean Spiny Lobsters walk the seabed all around the Caribbean and the Atlantic coast of the adjacent mainland.

Above: The long head appendages of spiny lobsters help them find prey, and keep in touch with their companions when migrating.

Christmas Island Red Crab

Gecarcoidea natalis

IUCN Not assessed

The crabs are the most familiar of the decapod crustaceans, and are noted for their sideways scuttle – a quick if peculiar way to get around, which works as well on land as it does underwater. Not all crabs live in or even near the sea, but they all need to return to it in order to spawn, as their larvae are always aquatic. For land crabs, this necessitates a journey, and for one kind of land crab in particular, the journey is quite literally traffic-stopping.

The traveller

Christmas Island lies in the Indian Ocean, 500km (310 miles) south of Indonesia. It is a three-pronged limestone island, about 134 sq km (52 sq miles), with steep cliffs forming most of its coastline, and a central plateau more than 300m (985ft) above sea-level. This geography makes perfect sense when you consider that it is the peak of a (mostly) underwater volcano. A couple of thousand people live on the island, and it is home to an array of endemic plants and animals – species found nowhere else on Earth.

Most isolated islands have – or had – many endemic species. These ecosystems are extremely fragile. The arrival of humans and the animals that come with them – pigs, rats, cats and other predators – often spells disaster, as the native species cannot cope and have nowhere to run. Christmas Island's flora and fauna has suffered fewer extinctions than most similar islands, thanks to its not being settled until the late 19th century, and the fact that most of it has long been protected as a national park. Among its special wildlife are 13 species of land crabs, including the famous Christmas Island Red Crab.

This is a big, robust crab that is usually bright red but can be orange or purple. It is very abundant on Christmas Island, with perhaps more than 20 million individuals roaming the island. There are also some Christmas Island Red Crabs on the much smaller Cocos Islands, but it occurs nowhere else on Earth.

These crabs are adapted to live on land – they retain their gills (these are located at the base of the legs in crustaceans) but can also extract oxygen from the air, thanks to an area around the gills which is rich in blood vessels and functions in the same way as lungs – this is the so-called branchiostegal lung. It allows the crabs to live in the rainforests of the island's interior, where they can be found in high concentrations, though they will also live on other parts of the island. They are active by day and forage on the forest floor, feeding mainly on plant material of all kinds that has fallen from the canopy but also scavenging carrion, raiding bins and occasionally taking live prey. Inevitably they encounter other crabs constantly but they are not social by nature at this time. During the dry season they enter a three-month phase of inactivity, shutting themselves inside a burrow in the ground (in a strictly one-crab-per-burrow arrangement) and plugging its entrance with a clump of dead leaves to minimise water loss.

The crabs are slow-growing and long-lived, helped in this second respect by a lack of natural predators on the island. They begin their lives on land at a tender age, spending just four weeks or so as marine larvae, but will not be ready to breed until they are about five years old. By this time the sexes are distinguishable, with males having bigger claws and females broader abdomens. In those first five years they moult several times a year but growth then slows down and moult becomes an annual event, completed while safely hidden in the forest burrow.

Beaches on Christmas Island become scenes of battle and romance when the crabs come to spawn.

Overleaf: Christmas Island is a remote tropical paradise for humans and crabs alike.

The journey

When the wet season begins in October to November, this is the trigger for all the crabs in breeding condition on Christmas Island to make their way to the spawning grounds. The journey can take them two and a half weeks, and is timed so that the females will be ready to lay their eggs during the last quarter of the moon – this is when there is the least difference between high and low tides, the best and safest time for them to make their trip to the sea to drop their eggs.

When more than 20 million crabs all migrate together, this is noticeable, to say the least, to everyone and everything else on the island. The crabs form moving red rivers that flow around or over obstacles along the path of least resistance, though they still have a steep downhill climb to tackle when they near the beaches. The biggest males arrive first and dig burrows, or fight other males to take over their burrows. When the females arrive, they seek out a burrow and mate with its resident male. The males then head back inland, while the females remain in the burrows. After about three days they lay their eggs and after another couple of weeks the eggs (which are tucked in a 'brood pouch' on the abdomen) are ready to be released into the sea. After a few days, virtually all the females will have completed their egg-laying and be on their way back to the island interior, followed a month later by a new generation of tiny baby crabs.

Migration is hazardous for the crabs. They risk dehydration by walking away from the damp safety of the rainforest, and if they are unlucky with the weather many will die. They also have to cross roads to reach the beaches. Park rangers spring into action at migration time, herding the crabs towards underpasses to keep them off the roads. A crab-friendly bridge has also been built across one of the key roads. This benefits crabs and humans alike – a large crab's carapace is tough enough to damage car tyres. Thanks to a sensitive attitude

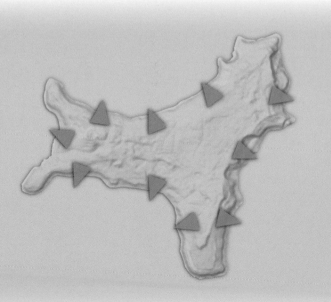

towards nature (and a desire to keep their cars in one piece), the Christmas Islanders are proud and respectful of their crabs and the wonder of their migration, despite the considerable inconvenience it causes.

There is some speculation that the crab's great abundance on Christmas Island is not natural but a consequence of the extinction of two endemic rat species, which might have kept its numbers down through predation. There is now a new predator on the block, which is making worrying inroads into the crab population. The alarmingly named Yellow Crazy Ant was accidentally introduced in the 1990s, and since then has brought the crab population down from an estimated 40 million to the 25 million or so of today – still plenty, you might think, but without urgent and decisive action the ant – a fearsome predator thanks to its ability to quickly establish huge 'super-colonies' – has the potential to wipe out the Christmas Island Red Crab, and make its extraordinary migrations a thing of the past.

Map: Crabs from across the island move towards the coastline in all directions every autumn.

Above: This charismatic little crustacean is much loved (and its eccentricities generously tolerated) by Christmas Islanders.

Image credits

Images by: 123rf.com (individual photographer in brackets) – page 19 (Andrea Izzotti); dreamstime.com (individual photographers in brackets) – front cover, page 38 (Zahorec), back cover, page 29 (Vladimir Melnikov), pages 2 (Emma Jones), 4–5 (Tomáš Bureš), 6 (Izanbar), 9 (Neal Cooper), 10, 135 (Cathy Keifer), 13 (Boppintheblues), 14 (Jocrebbin), 16–17 (Jandirkhansen), 21, 140 (Rinus Baak), 22, 24–25 (Vladimir Melnik), 27 (Aleksandrn), 30 (Wildair), 32–33 (Nadezhda Bolotina), 35 (Cecoffman), 37 (Johannes Gerhardus Swanepoel), 40–41 (Antonella865), 42 (Andreanita), 43 (Steffen Foerster), 44 (Audis4), 47, 58–59, 170–171 (Nico Smit), 49 (Reinout Van Wagtendonk), 50–51 (Anthony Aneese Totah Jr), 52 (Val Armstrong), 55 (Brett Critchley), 56 (Mun Lok Chan), 61 (Eng101), 63 (Daniel Schreiber), 64, 67 left (Lee Amery), 67 right (Buchsenmacher3), 69 (Steve Allen), 70 (Brian Kushner), 73 (Geoffrey Kuchera), 75, 134 (Mikelane45), 76 (Feathercollector), 79 (Mlarduengo), 82 (Ken Moore), 88 (Dmytro Pylypenko), 90–91 (Letloose78), 95, 121 (Brian Lasenby), 96 (Brian Kushner), 99 (Martin Ellis), 101 (Menno67), 102 (Leonidikan), 104–105 (Premekm), 107 (Ianmaton), 109 (Joan Egert), 110–111 (Broker), 115 (Scottamassey), 116 (Pcphotography69), 119 (Stephanie Rousseau), 122 (Jason Ondreicka), 125 (Wildphotos), 127 (Martyn Unsworth), 128 (Welshi23), 131 (Sigurbjorn Ragnarsson), 133 (Lukas Blazek), 137 (Mille19), 139 (Jerryway), 142–143 (Albertoloyo), 147 (Rosemarie Kappler), 148 (Dmitriy Goncharenko), 151 (Cliff Norton), 156–157 (Dennis Van De Water), 159, 161 (Wrangel), 162–163 (Paweł Opaska), 165 (Photographerlondon), 167 (Zhanghaobeibei), 168 (Paul Sparks), 173 (Shijianying), 175 (Andamanse), 176 (Carlo Ferraro), 179 (Allnaturalbeth), 181, 182, 184–185, 187 (Natador), 188 (Idreamphotos), 192 (Sunfe17); David Tipling – pages 81, 85, 87 and 93; and Frank Vassen – page 153.

Opposite: Humpback Whales can migrate thousands of kilometres each year.

Index

First published in 2016 by Reed New Holland Publishers Pty Ltd
London • Sydney • Auckland

The Chandlery, Unit 704, 50 Westminster Bridge Road, London SE1 7QY, UK
1/66 Gibbes Street, Chatswood, NSW 2067, Australia
5/39 Woodside Avenue, Northcote, Auckland 0627, New Zealand

www.newhollandpublishers.com

A record of this book is held at the British Library
and the National Library of Australia.

ISBN 978 1 92151 785 3

Managing Director: Fiona Schultz
Publisher and Project Editor: Simon Papps
Designer: Andrew Davies
Production Director: James Mills-Hicks
Printer: Times International Printers, Malaysia

10 9 8 7 6 5 4 3 2 1

Keep up with New Holland Publishers on Facebook
www.facebook.com/NewHollandPublishers